Little Ricky vs. Elvis vs. Ike

On Jan. 19, 1953, 44 million viewers tuned in to watch Lucy give birth to Little Ricky in the episode "Lucy Goes to the Hospital." The show's Nielsen rating was 71.7, meaning that 71.7 percent of all U.S. homes with TVs tuned in for the event, setting the record at the time for the highest viewership of a TV show. This record was broken in September 1956 when Elvis Presley (top right) first appeared on *The Ed Sullivan Show*.

The day after "Lucy Goes to the Hospital" aired, about 29 million people viewed President Dwight Eisenhower's (bottom right) inauguration. The country might have liked Ike, but they *loved* Lucy.

> ### "I'm not funny. What I am is brave."
>
> — **Lucille Ball**

Since its first run in 1953, *I Love Lucy* has never been off the air, has been viewed in more than

77

countries, and is dubbed in more than 22 languages.

300

size of the audience that attended each recording of *I Love Lucy*

181

number of episodes of *I Love Lucy* during its six-year run (including "The Pilot" episode).

40 Million

The estimated annual U.S. audience for reruns of *I Love Lucy.*

Mega Hit

	RANK	NIELSEN RATINGS*
Season 1 (1951-1952)	3	50.9
Season 2 (1952-1953)	1	67.3
Season 3 (1953-1954)	1	58.8
Season 4 (1954-1955)	1	49.3
Season 5 (1955-1956)	2	46.1
Season 6 (1956-1957)	1	43.7

* A Nielsen rating of 50.9 means that for Season 1, an average of 50.9% of all households with televisions at the time were watching *I Love Lucy*.

I Love Lucy

Classic Episodes

VITAMEATAVEGAMIN
FOR HEALTH

Profiles

Front Cover: Ronald Grant Archive
Back Cover: Photos by Everett Collection

We Love Lucy

Lucy and Ethel Buy the Same Dress

Chief Content Officer
June Kikuchi

Lucy Tells the Truth

Managing Editor
Ethan Mizer

Contributing Editor
Annika Geiger

Lucy Gets a Paris Gown

Art Director
Cindy Kassebaum

Lucy Does a Commercial

Multimedia Production Coordinator
Leah McGowan

Job Switching

Lucy Goes to the Rodeo

i-5 publishing

Chief Financial Officer
Nicole Fabian

Lucy is Enceinte

Chief Marketing Officer
Beth Freeman Reynolds

Redecorating

Chief Digital Officer
Jennifer Black-Glover

Chief Technology Officer
Kartik Money

Lucy and Superman

Sr. Vice President, I-5 Distribution
Scott Coffman

Lucy's Italian Movie

NPS Vice President, Sales & Marketing
Brian Theveny

The Camping Trip

Vice President, Direct Sales
Susan Roark

Job Switching

Book Division General Manager
Christopher Reggio

Ethel's Hometown

Multimedia Production Director
Laurie Panaggio

Lucy's Italian Movie

Design Director
Veronique Bos

First Stop

Editorial, Production and Corporate Office
3 Burroughs, Irvine, CA 92618
949-855-8822

I Love Lucy is published by I-5 Publishing, LLC, 3 Burroughs, Irvine, CA 92618-2804. Corporate headquarters located at 3 Burroughs, Irvine, CA 92618. ©2015 by I-5 Publishing, LLC. All rights reserved. Reproduction of any material from this issue in whole or in part is strictly prohibited.

Registration No. R126851765

Printed in the U.S.A.

FOREVER
Lucy

New generations find hilarity, relevance and timelessness in I Love Lucy *as they join the show's huge fanbase.*

BY CHAY LEMOINE

On Oct. 15, 1951, *I Love Lucy* premiered on CBS television. Since that time, the show has been in continual syndication, and millions and possibly billions of fans around the world have watched and rewatched the antics of Lucy, Ricky, Fred and Ethel.

And after more than 60 years, the world still loves Lucy. For proof, just look to social media. The *I Love Lucy* Facebook page has close to 2 million likes, 80 percent of which are from women, which may not be surprising. However, what is startling is the age range of these women: 21 percent are 13 to 24 in age, 20 percent are 25 to 34, 11 percent are 35 to 44, 16 percent are 45 to 55, and 12 percent are 55 or older.

STILL LAUGHING

There's an obvious reason why *I Love Lucy* is still popular with teens, young adults, adults and seniors. It's funny! Even with repeated viewings, the sitcom still hits the right notes. Many Lucy addicts have seen their favorite episodes hundreds of times, and they still howl with laughter even though they know the episodes by heart.

I Love Lucy offers the perfect combination of physical comedy and good, solid writing, resulting in some of the funniest moments on TV. Who can forget Lucy's fight with the Italian winemakers in "Lucy's Italian Movie," the iconic candy-factory routine with Ethel in "Job Switching" and the classic Vitameatavegamin pitch in "Lucy Does a TV Commercial"? These episodes get funnier with each viewing. Even the most jaded and sophisticated viewer can't help but see the humor in Lucy's ability to make the most exaggerated slapstick seem believable and funny.

In the early years of the show, three writers — Jess Oppenheimer, Madelyn Pugh and Bob Carroll Jr. — composed an episode's script in just one week. The casts' performances elevated great writing into classic comedy. The actors made it all seem so easy, and viewers believed that Lucille Ball, Desi Arnaz, William Frawley and

I Love Lucy's relatable cast and plot make the show timeless.

Vivian Vance were exactly who they seemed to be on screen. Talent like that doesn't go out of style; it becomes classic and iconic.

By utilizing universally shared situations like marriage, the show tickled viewers' funny bones. For example, when Lucy thought Ricky was seeing another woman, Ethel dismissed the idea. Lucy says, "If some woman were trying to take Fred away from you, you'd sing another tune!" Ethel replies, "Yeah: 'Happy Days are Here Again.'"

In another episode, Ricky finds money in Lucy's purse, and she tells him, "It's my mad money." When Ricky counts out $200, Lucy adds, "Yeah, I get awful mad."

RELATABLE AT EVERY STAGE

I Love Lucy was a product of its time, but the show addressed issues that remain relevant today, which is probably why the show continues to be popular. Several of the show's plots resonate with today's female viewers. The episode titled "Equal Rights" depicts Ricky asserting that he is "king of the castle," the prevailing mindset of the period. This outburst causes Lucy to demand that she be given equal rights. The Ricardos and the Mertzes go out for dinner, and the men decide to teach the women a lesson by insisting that they pay for their share of the meal. Although Lucy and Ethel have to wash dishes because they don't have money, the women have the upper hand by the end of the show after Ricky and Fred are arrested.

In every instance, Lucy's feminine wiles overcome Ricky's masculine posturing. Lucy is strong-willed and beautiful. She has a handsome husband, a beautiful baby and dreams of a career in show business. If she wants something, she doesn't hesitate to get it even if it causes a conflict with current social conventions.

Different generations of woman may discover Lucy at different times in their lives, but for fans young and old, the appeal of the program doesn't seem to diminish.

Very young viewers identify with Lucy's childlike qualities and her sense of play. When Lucy cries, she cries like a child. She pouts and whines and will annoy Ricky until she gets her way, much like a misbehaving child.

As viewers age and enter their awkward adolescent years, they can identify with Lucy's struggle for identity. She can't sing, she can't dance, she can't tell a joke, she burns food in the kitchen, she is clumsy and awkward, and she often makes a bad first impression. The message here for young teens: Behind the ugly duckling is the beautifully talented swan. Lucy provides hope because she ultimately prevails over all of her critics.

When Lucy fans start families, they can see themselves in Lucy as she struggles to take care of a home, a child and a husband. Lucy also deals with keeping the romance alive in her marriage — another relatable topic for women today. In the episode titled "The Girls Want to Go to the Nightclub," Lucy exclaims, "Ever since we said 'I do,' there are so many things we don't."

In Fred and Ethel's marriage, we see the reflection of a relationship that lost its spark long ago. As Ethel says in "The Camping Trip" episode, "Our honeymoon was over on our honeymoon!"

CONTROVERSY

In the 1950s, when *I Love Lucy* premiered, the Ricardos' interracial marriage was so unusual that it seemed to exist merely for comedic effect. But what was considered highly uncommon then is considered part of the norm today.

The world of *I Love Lucy* is not the same one we find in *Ozzie and Harriet* (1952 to 1966) or *Leave it to Beaver* (1957 to 1963), where domestic strife is mild. Ricky and Lucy have noisy and loud conflicts — and in two languages. Contemporary viewers see the intercultural bickering between the Ricardos as real and relevant. Except for the mocking of Ricky's fracturing of the English language, the Cuban culture is embraced and celebrated on the show.

Besides the interracial pairing of Lucy and Ricky, the show also depicts the May/December relationship of their neighbors Ethel and Fred. The show's portrayal of their marriage makes it seems as if the age difference was planned. In reality, it was the result of accidental casting. Gale Gordon, an actor with whom Ball had worked in the past and who played Mr. Mooney on her later TV series *The Lucy Show*, was originally tapped to play Fred.

Bea Benaderet, who played Lucy's friend on her radio series *My Favorite Husband* and later went on to play the mother in Petticoat Junction, was eyed for the role of Ethel. However, both had other commitments, and the producers found other candidates. Gordon and Benaderet were

Lucille Ball played to the audience with her over-the-top facial expressions (top). The magic of the show was the love and creativity between the on-screen and real-life husband-and-wife team.

Colorization and Its Discontents

Lucy purists have sometimes disagreed, but there is little doubt that efforts by CBS to colorize episodes of *I Love Lucy* have introduced a new set of fans to the series. For those who view the black-and-white episodes as less than entertaining, a few selected episodes are now available in living color.

The coloring of iconic episodes has allowed for the colorization of *Lucy* merchandise. Calendars, coffee mugs and T-shirts all come alive in the eyes of contemporary audiences when Lucy's red hair is given the star treatment. It's unlikely that all of the episodes will be colorized due to the expense, so for purists, black and white will continue to be the norm.

Though Vance and Frawley reportedly did not get along off-stage, they were consummate professionals on-screen.

closer in age, and the age difference of the on-screen couple would have been lost.

The May/December casting worked well with both the original and modern audiences, but it caused conflict between Frawley and Vance. After viewers accepted the Mertzes' relationship, Vance felt insulted that fans so readily believed her marriage to Frawley, who was more than 20 years older than her. She sometimes took her frustrations out on him, and Frawley responded in kind, offering even more Fred Mertz insults to be added to the script.

OLD YET TIMELESS

I Love Lucy shows aspects of 1950s life that are unfamiliar or at least uncommon today — such as Ricky sitting by the landline telephone waiting for Hollywood to call, Lucy and Ricky smoking cigarettes — and while viewers today may chuckle at these set props, they are more interested in the relationships between the four main characters.

I Love Lucy's fanbase continues to grow because the show was and still is funny and relevant thanks to brilliant comedic writing and star performances from the four actors who portrayed the Ricardos and the Mertzes.

Even watching the show in black and white has a profound advantage with today's audiences. Without bright colors and special effects, viewers are forced to focus on the humor and the performances. The black-and-white format also allows viewers to escape into a kinder and simpler time where happy endings do exist. That the show has survived and thrived through different generations' multiple perspectives and cultural assumptions is a testament to its longevity and groundbreaking nature.

Lucy Ricardo is obsessed with getting into show business, celebrity, fashion and entertainment. Sound familiar? The social-media generation understands *Lucy* because it follows these same things. They're fashionistas and would-be reality-show stars or YouTubers, who can easily understand maxing out their credit cards. There

may be a disconnect between today's viewers and other older sitcoms, but *I Love Lucy* remains remarkably relevant.

Lucy love is felt around the world. From T-shirts and chocolates to office stationery and lunchboxes, you can find *I Love Lucy* merchandise and collectibles all over the Internet. And that's not all. An *I Love Lucy* tribute at Universal Studios Florida has been running for more than 20 years. And the Lucille Ball Comedy Festival in Ball's hometown of Jamestown, N.Y., has attracted tens of thousands of attendees for close to 25 years. *I Love Lucy* is an iconic piece of American pop culture. 📺

Chay Lemoine is a professor at Southern Illinois University and teaches and writes about I Love Lucy. *His favorite episode is "L.A. at Last!" (see page 34).*

LUCY DOES A TV COMMERCIAL

SEASON: 1

EPISODE: 30

ORIGINAL AIR DATE: MAY 5, 1952

PLOT

Ricky is hosting a TV show and needs someone to star in a commercial. When Lucy finds out, she begs for the job. Ricky refuses, so she decides to convince him to let her star in the commercial. Later, when Ricky returns home, Fred flips a sheet to uncover the Ricardos' television set, revealing Lucy's face in the TV. She does a mock commercial for Philip Morris, stopping only when Ricky plugs in the TV and almost electrocutes her.

The next morning, Lucy tricks Ricky, Fred and the woman cast to star in the commercial: Lucy finds out when and where the commercial is shooting and tells the woman she's no longer needed. Lucy then goes to the studio to shoot the commercial.

The director and a stagehand explain the product they're advertising. It's a tonic called Vitameatavegamin, and it contains meat, vegetables, minerals and vitamins. What Lucy doesn't know is that it also contains 23 percent alcohol.

They begin the rehearsal, with Lucy taking sips of the tonic as she rehearses. At first she hates the flavor and makes comical faces with each sip. Over time, however, she begins to enjoy the taste of Vitameatavegamin. Lucy soon begins to feel the effects of the alcohol, forgetting her lines, slurring her words and flubbing the name of the tonic. The director becomes concerned and suggests that Lucy rest before the show begins.

Lucy reappears later, still feeling the alcohol, as Ricky performs a song on stage. Lucy stumbles around the stage and imitates Ricky's singing until he finally picks her up and removes her from the stage.

Trivia

- Vivian Vance does not appear in this episode. Fred explains to Lucy that she's visiting her mother.

- Lucille Ball called this her favorite episode.

- According to a photo of the original Vitameatavegamin bottle, the tonic's alcohol content was 11 percent, not the 23 percent mentioned in the episode. During rehearsals, the number was raised for dramatic effect.

"Do you pop out at parties? Are you unpoopular?"

About filming the episode, Ross Elliott, who played the director, said: "I chewed the inside of my mouth to keep from laughing out loud. Lucy would do new stuff that wasn't rehearsed, like an extra-funny face. Then, at one point, she became 'drunk' and started making eyes at me, flirting, and I almost broke up again."

Classic Episode

JOB SWITCHING
SEASON: 2
EPISODE: 1
ORIGINAL AIR DATE: Sept. 15, 1952

PLOT

An angry Ricky discovers that Lucy has overdrawn her bank account yet again. An argument ensues over who has it worse: men, who have to work, or women, who take care of the home. Fred and Ethel get involved, and the four of them agree to switch roles for a week: The men will cook and clean at home while the women go to work.

Lucy and Ethel visit an employment office and are sent to work at Kramer's Kandy Kitchen where Lucy's first assignment is to dip chocolates while Ethel boxes them up. Lucy tries to befriend the woman working next to her, but they end up fighting instead, with each smearing chocolate all over the other woman.

Back at home, Ricky and Fred ruin their wives' clothes by ironing them and agree to cook dinner and dessert together for the four of them. Fred's seven-layer cake looks like a pancake, and Ricky's cooked chickens wind up on the ceiling and his pot of rice overflows all over the kitchen.

At the candy factory, Lucy and Ethel have been assigned a new task: take chocolates from a conveyor belt, wrap them and place them back on the belt. If they fail, they will be fired.

At first, the job seems easy. Soon, though, Lucy and Ethel struggle to keep up. They shove chocolates in their shirts and hats, as well as in their mouths to make it look like they've wrapped them all.

A sick-looking Lucy and Ethel arrive home, where the kitchen is a disaster. They admit they were fired, and Ricky and Fred acknowledge that they failed at housekeeping. To show their appreciation for their wives' hard work, the husbands bought their wives a gift: 5 pounds of chocolate!

Trivia

- Ricky's fall on the rice-covered floor was unscripted. It caused him to bruise his ribs.

- The woman rolling chocolate next to Lucy was an actual candy maker who was uncomfortable speaking on camera, so her lines were cut from the scene.

"Let her roll!"
— Chocolate factory supervisor

In the scene where Lucy and the woman working next to her smear chocolate on each other, it looks like they do it twice. It was actually one shot taken from two angles and shown twice.

Elvia Allman played the candy-factory boss. She guest-starred on *I Love Lucy* several times before being given a recurring role on *The Lucy-Desi Comedy Hour.*

THE *Lucy* TEAM

The creative forces — actors, writers, producers and directors — worked collaboratively to bring America's favorite TV show to life.

BY ELISA JORDAN

When *I Love Lucy* was first broadcast, millions of Americans were introduced to four characters that soon became like family members — Ricky and Lucy Ricardo and their landlords and best friends, Fred and Ethel Mertz. Since then, the sitcom has entertained generations and shows no signs of going away any time soon.

The four cast members — Lucille Ball, Desi Arnaz, Vivian Vance and William Frawley — made the show look effortless, but it took an entire team of talented people collaborating every week to bring Lucy Ricardo's wacky adventures into American homes.

RADIO ROOTS

The roots of *I Love Lucy* started with the CBS radio show *My Favorite Husband* (1948 to 1951). The show starred Lucille Ball and Richard Denning as a well-to-do couple, but when writers Jess Oppenheimer, Bob Carroll Jr. and Madelyn Pugh came aboard, the trio reworked the premise and turned the fictional George and Liz Cooper into a middle-class couple to make them more accessible to listeners. The concept worked, and CBS decided to bring the show to television.

"TV was going to be the 'next big thing,'" said cultural and Hollywood historian Amy Condit, who has contributed to "Film Noir Fanatics" segments on Turner Classic Movies and documentaries on Walt Disney and Buster Keaton. "From 1949 to1950, the number of television sets in existence quadrupled

William Frawley, Vivian Vance, Lucille Ball and Desi Arnaz pose with the crew that brought *I Love Lucy* to life each week.

Three Bobs and a Babe

During the 1955 to 1956 season, Bob Carroll and Madelyn Pugh were joined by two more writers. They also both happened to share the same first name as Carroll, and they were at one point jokingly referred to as "three Bobs and a babe."

"Bob Schiller and Bob Weiskopf joined the series ... and wrote for the final two seasons of the half-hour shows and all the way through the Lucy-Desi hour specials, which ended in 1960," said Tom Gilbert, co-author of *Desilu: The Story of Lucille Ball and Desi Arnaz*. "They beautifully adapted to what was by then a hugely successful formula. They did it so well, it was hard to tell who wrote what after they joined the team."

"The two Bobs were brought in to give some new life to the show and help out the other writers," said Rick Carl, a Lucille Ball historian. "Everyone would sit in Jess Oppenheimer's office until a story emerged. They would work backwards, conjuring up a final block comedy scene and then finally reaching that scene logically. It was not an easy task."

from 1 million to 4 million, and CBS knew that TV was going to blossom in a big way."

With television on the rise, studios were desperate to find fresh material — or adapt existing content from other sources.

"*My Favorite Husband* was not just an influence; it was the direct inspiration and precursor to *I Love Lucy*," said Rick Carl, a Lucille Ball historian. Carl is a founding member of the *I Love Lucy* fan club, co-producer and art director for the Loving Lucy conventions, and consultant for *I Love Lucy*-related documentaries.

Bringing the writers over from the radio show seemed like a natural choice to get things started. The radio show was already a success, so it stood to reason that the same team could perform similar magic for TV.

"Jess Oppenheimer, Madelyn Pugh and Bob Carroll Jr. … all worked on the radio program, and several of the early episodes of *I Love Lucy* were based on episodes of *My Favorite Husband*," said Cindy DeLaHoz, author of the books *Lucy at the Movies* and *The Lucille Ball Treasures.*

There was an extra benefit to retooling the radio show. Because television was new and *I Love Lucy* would utilize cutting-edge technology for the era, many details still had to be worked out.

"When Madelyn, Bob and Jess started writing [for *I Love Lucy*] in June 1951, the specific method of filming was still unresolved, so the three were concocting scripts that would play as if done 'live,' stories that required a minimum of costume changes, sets and complicated physical business," Condit said.

From there, changes were made to the characters themselves. Gone were George and Liz Cooper. The TV couple was very different — the husband was tailored to fit Desi Arnaz.

"The basic framework for *I Love Lucy* — a wacky housewife versus a more staid husband, with an older married couple as sidekicks — came from the radio show," said Tom Gilbert, journalist and author of *Desilu: The Story of Lucille Ball and Desi Arnaz*. "It was then altered to accommodate Desi Arnaz in the role of the husband. Because he was Cuban-born with a thick accent, he wouldn't be believable as a banker, so the character was made a bandleader, which Desi was in real life. Many other changes were necessitated as a result."

The Remarkable
Desi Arnaz

Desi Arnaz got along with everyone both personally and professionally. "Everyone loved Desi," said Tom Gilbert, co-author of *Desilu: The Story of Lucille Ball and Desi Arnaz.*

Arnaz was, in essence, the glue that held all the elements of *I Love Lucy* together, whether that be the cast, crew, production or even the running of the studio. His ability to respect writers' talents, boost Lucy's confidence so she could give her best performance, and negotiate on behalf of Desilu Productions is nothing short of remarkable.

He famously had a photographic memory, which helped him accomplish his many duties on the set and keep the show running.

THE CREATIVE CENTER

At the show's creative heart were the writers — Oppenheimer, Pugh and Carroll. Oppenheimer also served as producer, and was, Carl said, "the creative force" behind the show, something Ball herself acknowledged when she called him "the brains" of *I Love Lucy*.

It was also Oppenheimer who was responsible for creating many of *I Love Lucy*'s noteworthy elements. "When developing the pilot episode for *I Love Lucy* in 1950, it was Jess who suggested that Desi play a 'working stiff' bandleader and Lucy be his zany wife whose greatest wish is to break into show business," said DeLaHoz.

"Jess contributed a lot to the series both as producer and head writer," Gilbert said. "But to me, his greatest contribution was the child-like quality he imbued in the Lucy Ricardo character ... which had its genesis in his earlier writing for Fanny Brice's classic 'Baby Snooks' persona."

Although some of the early episodes of *I Love Lucy* were retooled plots from *My Favorite Husband*, Pugh and Carroll were soon off and running, coming up with original ideas, scripts and wacky adventures. The fun was also hard work. The writing duo worked as many as 70 hours per week coming up with ideas and putting jokes on paper, Carl said.

At Monday morning conferences their ideas were reviewed; when an idea was selected, the writers would start developing it. "They would plot an episode with Jess Oppenheimer, often spending the entire day outlining the story, scene by scene, laugh by laugh," Carl said.

Pictured from left at the buffet table during a 1955 *I Love Lucy* press party are Vivian Vance, Jess Oppenheimer (producer and writer for the show), Lucille Ball and Desi Arnaz. Along with the show's writers, Oppenheimer has been described as the creative heart of *I Love Lucy*.

"Then they would take all the information necessary to the plot and weave it into the story so it would flow naturally."

Once a concept was chosen, Carroll and Pugh would write a first draft and deliver it to Oppenheimer, sometimes even dropping it off in his home mailbox, Gilbert said. Oppenheimer would then go through the script, making notes, smoothing over points and making sure the tone was consistent with the other episodes.

Pugh and Carroll would incorporate Oppenheimer's suggestions and hand in a new draft. "[Jess] would do a final 'polish' and would dictate the entire script from start to finish on a dictation machine," Carl said. "In his position, Jess needed to know every aspect of the script so that if a question arose at any time during the production, he knew the reason why something was in there."

A COLLABORATIVE PROCESS

Arnaz proved to be an ideal collaborator. What made the atmosphere on the set so special was in part the fact that Arnaz implicitly trusted his creative team. This gave them the freedom needed to produce their best material. Arnaz was a great "script doctor," as Ball called him, and easily spotted plot holes, Gilbert said.

"Desi trusted and, most importantly, nurtured the writers," he added. "If he didn't like something in the script, he coddled them into fixing it. They were charmed by Desi and valued his opinion."

Indeed, when praise was appropriate, Arnaz was forthcoming. When critiquing was necessary, he was a master at gently making suggestions so no one's feelings were hurt.

Ball also trusted Arnaz and deferred to his opinion. Arnaz paid attention to how the writers worked, noticed how they tested out the jokes and stunts, and had a keen instinct for how Ball's comedic skills worked. At times, Ball would worry that certain plots wouldn't work or was afraid to try something. Without his encouragement, Ball might not have per-

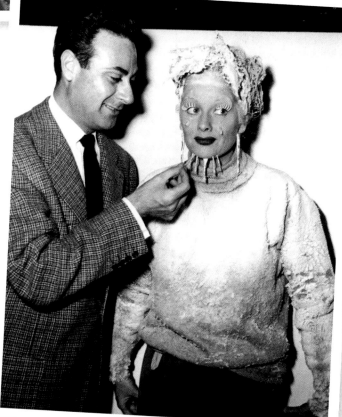

Writers Madelyn Pugh and Bob Carroll Jr. (shown in 1981 in the top photo) would often imagine Lucy and the gang in some zany situation or precarious position and then construct the plot backward from that premise.

Without Desi Arnaz's encouragement, Ball might not have performed some of Lucy's more outlandish stunts.

Lucy & Ethel:
Best Friends On and Off Screen

In the beginning, Lucille Ball had a particular vision of what Ethel Mertz should look like — and Vivian Vance didn't fit that vision.

"With the right clothing and make-up, Vivian could be made to look 20 years older than Lucy," said Amy Condit, a cultural and Hollywood historian. "Lucy forbade Vivian from wearing false eyelashes and had it written into Vivian's contract that she would remain 20 pounds over-weight during the filming season. However, Lucy went out of her way to relax Vivian on the first day of filming."

With time, Ball realized that Vance was the per-fect "accomplice" for the duo's onscreen antics. Their relationship deepened into a warm professional and personal one. They worked together until 1977, when Vance had a stroke, Condit said.

formed many of Lucy Ricardo's crazy stunts.

"It's hard to imagine, but as funny as Lucy was as an actress, she didn't innately know what was funny — on paper, at least," Gilmore said. "Desi helped her a lot with that. He knew what would work for her, and he also knew that the scripts had to maintain a thread of believability — no matter how preposterous the situation Lucy found herself in. And he was a stickler for that believability. Lucy mainly worried about looking like a fool, which she had every right to fear. Not many performers could pull off the outrageous stuff she did without looking silly or forced."

Arnaz greatly appreciated Pugh and Carroll's willingness to test stunts before presenting them to Oppenheimer and the rest of the cast. By the time Arnaz, Ball, Frawley and Vance read the script, many of the possible kinks had already been worked out.

For instance, in the episode where Lucy and Ricky are handcuffed together, Carroll and Pugh really handcuffed themselves to each other during the writing process to figure out what worked, what didn't and exactly how the actors needed to move for maximum laughter.

There were other instances, too. Pugh was in the unique position of being a female writer — rare at the time — and because she was writing for a female comedic lead, she made the ideal "stand-in" for Lucy during the creative process. This improved and refined the scriptwriting.

"In the 'Tennessee Bound' episode where they end up in Ernie Ford's hometown, the

From Real to Reel

Desi Arnaz and Lucille Ball were directly involved in the scriptwriting for *I Love Lucy*, with Arnaz checking everything over to make sure it was suitable and (somewhat) believable, no matter how absurd the plotline. But sometimes Ball and Arnaz were indirectly responsible for the plots that appeared in the show. The ever eagle-eyed writers would sometimes take inspiration from the real-life couple.

"As the company spent a lot of time at the studio and became close, on occasion, incidents in the Arnazes lives would influence the writers and show up in a script," Lucille Ball historian Rick Carl said. "An example of this was Lucy's love of fresh air at night while sleeping, where Desi wanted it warm and toasty. This was the direct inspiration for the scene in 'Breaking The Lease,' where the Ricardos try to outsmart each other by continuing to open and close the window before going to bed that night.

"The writers were lucky to capitalize on their knowledge of Lucy and Desi's real-life characteristics and carefully tailored their material at times. Knowing, for instance, that Lucille Ball was superstitious and knocked on wood, they wrote the script for 'The Séance,' in which Lucy spoiled a business deal for Ricky by consulting a horoscope. The fact that Lucy liked to imitate Tallulah Bankhead, Bob (Carroll) and Madelyn (Pugh) wrote a sequence in 'Lucy Fakes Illness,' where Mrs. Ricardo imagines herself as the famous actress," Carl said.

original idea was for there to be a big taffy pull in the final scene, during which the gang wraps the sheriff and his twin daughters up in the taffy and escape," Gilbert said. "Bob and Madelyn tried it and found out that the taffy fell apart and wouldn't work. So they changed it to a rope and a square dance. Madelyn tried out the 'flaming nose' from the William Holden episode so Lucille wouldn't be hurt. They also considered rolling Lucy up in a rug for a comic bit, but when Madelyn tried it, she almost suffocated, so the idea was ditched."

Ever the good sport, Pugh was also locked in a steamer trunk and stuck in a loving cup, Condit said. "She also glued icicles to her face, filled her blouse with eggs and tried wrapping chocolate bonbons at breakneck speed."

BRINGING LUCY TO LIFE

Once the plots and details were worked out, it was the actors' responsibility to breathe life into the jokes on the page. Buoyed by Desi's positivity and support, Ball was capable of extraordinary comedic feats. Their bond was

In The Director's Chair

Although there was more than one director who worked on *I Love Lucy*, the man who sat in the director's chair most often was William "Bill" Asher, who later went on to find considerable success as the producer of all eight seasons of *Bewitched* with his then-wife, Elizabeth Montgomery.

Asher directed episodes 39-127, an epic run that included the famous "Job Switching" and Hollywood episodes. His job wasn't always easy — directing the show was a delicate combination of creating art and technical precision.

"Asher's creativity was his innate ability to watch the floor and ensure that all cameras and actors hit their marks at the required moments," said Rick Carl, an *I Love Lucy* historian. "Precision was crucial, as nobody wanted to stop a performance in front of the audience. He rarely asked for pick-ups and when they did, it was usually a guest star who forgot a line."

Things got off to a rocky start between Asher and Lucille Ball, who initially didn't trust the director and overrode his decisions on the set and told the other actors what to do, said Tom Gilbert, author of *Desilu: The Story of Lucille Ball and Desi Arnaz.*

Asher knew he had to put a stop to this, so he confronted her, and Ball fled the set in tears.

"[Bill] was so new he didn't even have an office yet, so he went to the men's room to ponder what he had just done, and started to cry," Gilbert said. "Desi came in and told Bill he was right to confront Lucy, and things went pretty well from then on. Lucille came to trust Bill, but occasionally, when tasked with a particularly outlandish stunt, would quip, 'Would you ask *your* wife to do this?'"

William Asher (right) with wife Elizabeth Montgomery, the actress who played Samantha on the show *Bewitched*.

> *Pugh was in the unique position of being a female writer – rare at the time – and because she was writing for a female comedic lead, she made the ideal "stand-in" for Lucy during the creative process.*

such that, even when their marriage began to crumble, their chemistry remained on screen so the audience never knew that there was marital strife in private.

Similarly, the on-screen chemistry between the Ricardos' sidekicks, the Mertzes, was just as strong. The dynamics between the four actors created magic on screen, but things weren't always idyllic behind the scenes.

Vance and Frawley often had difficulty getting along. The character of Fred was a curmudgeon, so it lent some authenticity to the role when Frawley and Vance struggled in real life. It didn't always make things easy, though.

"Vivian considered herself to be sophisticated and glamorous in real life and hated the idea of people believing she could be married to 'that fat old man,'" Gilbert said. "Bill Frawley, who had sung in vaudeville, thought Vivian was full of herself and made fun of her singing. There wasn't really an open animosity, but they didn't relish hanging out together. Whatever tension there was played well on screen, as they were always putting each other down."

Much has been made over the idea that Vivian and Bill "hated" each other. They were hardly best friends, but creating the best show possible was priority No. 1 for all involved — and the actors at the heart of *I Love Lucy* were all seasoned professionals first and foremost.

TIMELESS TELEVISION

The result of everyone's creativity and hard work? Lightning in a bottle. The show continues to make new generations of fans laugh. Those scripts that were dropped off in mailboxes, stunts that were worked out ahead of time and the dedication of the cast created something timeless. "*I Love Lucy* possesses that rare combination of superior writing and credible acting, which keeps the shows fresh," Carl said.

According to Carl, when interviewers asked Ball about the secret to her popularity and the amazing longevity of her television shows, she never hesitated to answer, "my writers!" "After the 100th episode of *I Love Lucy*," Carl said, "Lucy expressed [her appreciation for the writers] to the entire company, 'I love them dearly, I appreciate them daily, I praise them hourly, and I thank God for them every night!'"

Elisa Jordan is a journalist who writes and speaks on Hollywood history. She also regularly serves as script editor for numerous documentaries on Southern California. Her favorite episode is "L.A. at Last!" (see page 34).

Madelyn Pugh often tried Lucy's stunts first to make sure they were safe.

LUCY IS ENCEINTE

SEASON: 2
EPISODE: 10
ORIGINAL AIR DATE: Dec. 8, 1952

PLOT

Lucy unexpectedly finds out she is expecting and has a romantic plan to tell Ricky when he comes home for lunch. However, everything goes awry because Ricky is having a stressful day at the club, and Lucy is interrupted by phone calls and the Mertzes knocking at the door.

When Ricky rushes back to the club to take care of an emergency, Lucy is dejected. She goes to the Tropicana determined to tell Ricky that he's going to be a father, but again she is interrupted — this time by various people asking for Ricky's opinion on lighting, seating, etc., during rehearsal.

That evening during his show, Ricky is handed a note, asking him to sing "We're Having a Baby, My Baby and Me," because someone in the audience has yet to tell her husband about their "blessed event." As Ricky walks around the audience singing and asking couples if they are the expectant pair, he sees Lucy, who nods. Ricky continues to sing until it dawns on him that he is going to be a father. He rushes to Lucy's side and shouts, "It's me!"

In the episode following "Lucy is Enceinte," Lucy feels neglected, so Ricky takes her dancing at the club and sings "Cheek to Cheek" to her.

While singing "Rock-a-bye Baby," Desi Arnaz mistakenly sings "the cradle will fall" line twice. Because his reaction was so natural, they did not do another take.

Trivia

- Both Lucy and Ricky are crying as the episode ends — the tears were real!

- Lucille Ball was five months pregnant when the episode was filmed.

"We are?! Oh, isn't that wonderful? I never had a baby before!"

— Ethel, upon hearing Lucy say, "We're going to have a baby!"

Ball and Arnaz's first decade of marriage was childless — just like the Ricardos'. Arnaz's mother said that because they had not been married in a church, they weren't blessed with children. So the couple renewed their vows in 1949, and two years later and after three miscarriages, the Arnazes welcomed their daughter, Lucie.

LUCY TELLS THE TRUTH
SEASON: 3
EPISODE: 6
ORIGINAL AIR DATE: Nov. 9, 1953

PLOT

While the Mertzes and Ricky sit around discussing their past exploits in show business, Lucy can't help but be jealous. She insists that she has been in show business. She tells them that she was in Oklahoma, claiming to have been the star, then a featured player, then a chorus girl, right down to a ticket taker.

Just then, flowers arrive for Ricky. Surprised, he asks who would send them, and Lucy says that she told some friends she and Ricky couldn't have dinner with them because he sprained his ankle. Ricky and the Mertzes proceed to taunt Lucy about her inability to tell the truth. They bet her $100 she can't go an entire day without lying.

At a bridge game the next day, Lucy finds ways around telling the truth, but after Ethel goads her into it, Lucy decides to be totally blunt. Back at home, Lucy reveals how freeing it is to be totally honest. Lucy proceeds to lay into Fred and Ricky. When she describes Ricky, she tells him he's a coward because he's afraid that if she gets a break in show business, she'll be the big star in the family.

Ricky then tells her she can come along with him to an audition that night. When Lucy runs off to get ready, Ricky shares his scheme with the Mertzes: Without experience, Lucy won't be taken seriously, and if she lies about her experience to get the job, they'll win the bet.

At the audition, Lucy won't lie to get the job and risk losing the bet. However, when another performer, a man with a cape, begins speaking in Italian about his assistant not being there for the audition, Lucy volunteers, saying she can speak Italian.

As she confusedly tries to dance with the performer, he becomes aggravated and forces her to stand inside a silhouette with balloons around it. Then he starts throwing knives at her. Lucy is scared stiff as the balloons pop around her. Finally, he puts a cigarette in her mouth and is about to swipe it with a knife, when Lucy breaks down screaming for Ricky.

She admits she can't speak Italian and agrees to pay the bet. Ricky then shows her that the board she was standing against is a trick setup; the knives release safely from the back. Realizing she lost the bet and her chance to be in a show, Lucy begins to wail.

In episode 61, the Ricardos switched apartments to number 3B to get an extra room for Little Ricky. In this episode, the number is changed to 3D so that Lucy's statement that she appeared in "3D" when asked about her experience would work.

"*You can't tell people the truth – they think you're lying. You have to lie to make them think you're telling the truth.*"

— Lucy

Trivia

- In the original script, the final act involved Lucy finding out Ricky lied on his income tax return, but Desi Arnaz wouldn't have it. He didn't want anyone to think that a Cuban immigrant would lie to the United States government. He insisted on a rewrite, and the knife-throwing scene was added to fill the space.

THE *Lucy* MYSTIQUE

I Love Lucy impacted America's perception of women, marriage, comedy and feminism.

BY LORI LANDAY

I *Love Lucy* played — and continues to play — a momentous role in American culture. During the 1950s, it had an enormous impact on how the television industry, sitcom genre and audience developed during this formative period. *I Love Lucy* redefined what popular meant and affected pop culture as a whole. Its depictions of marriage, home life, gender and ethnicity influenced the American zeitgeist. Today, *I Love Lucy* shapes how we look at and remember the past. When we put all of these aspects together, we may have the most significant and beloved television phenomenon ever.

At the center of the sensation was and is Lucille Ball, whose character, Lucy Ricardo, set the precedent for many characters in other TV shows and movies following the original run of the series. No other television actress has been as beloved as Ball, perhaps because of the "housewife" role she played at the

Lucy's problems, such as issues with budgeting, may be stereotypical, but her ways of dealing with them and Ricky subvert viewers' expectations.

Lucy is a housewife who doesn't want to be just a housewife, a desire that the character expresses and enacts to comic effect.

Although what we remember most from *I Love Lucy* are the outrageous stunts and unrealistic setups — like Lucy doing a commercial for Vitameatavegamin or Lucy and Ethel dressing up as Martians on the top of the Empire State Building — the show focused on aspects of everyday life to which its audience related, like marriage, work, living on a budget, having a baby and friendships with neighbors.

Of course, some of these topics were already familiar from radio shows, comic strips and theatrical comedy going back to its roots in Italian Commedia dell'arte. This theatrical form featured tricks to get money, mistaken identities, physical comedy and dramatic comedy that included character archetypes, such as the tricky slave, going as far back as ancient Greek plays.

What was new about how these familiar themes of comedy were treated in *I Love Lucy* is that they were on television, edited based on conventions familiar from the language of film. Because the show was broadcast weekly into people's homes over months, and then years, the characters and settings became a part of what people saw in their own homes and familiar in a way that those from film, radio or live theater were not.

For example, in the pilot for *I Love Lucy*, we see Ricky shaving as if the camera were the mirror. Television shows did not usually put viewers in such a direct and intimate point of view. Viewers were inserted into the domestic life of the show's characters from the beginning, and the series brought an idealized representation of home life into their homes.

Audiences responded to what they saw in the Ricardo home and made *I Love Lucy* the most popular television show of the time. Several factors combined to create the success:

beginning of television culture in America at a time when Americans were focused on home life after World War II.

FITTING INTO CONVENTION

Lucy is a housewife who doesn't want to be just a housewife, a desire that the character expresses and enacts to comic effect. Because she is "Lucy," who always has a zany, screwball scheme, her attempts to address her dissatisfaction within typical social domestic constraints fuel the comic situations the character creates. Ball's extraordinary comedic talents and deft understanding of physical comedy are given the opportunity to shine in these circumstances.

the visible chemistry between real-life spouses Lucille Ball and Desi Arnaz, Ball's fantastic comedic ability, four strong actors in the lead roles and excellent writing. Mixing standard comedy conventions from film and radio with the novel and innovative pushed the show over the top.

At the time, a mixed marriage between a Cuban and an American was not something most people were used to seeing on TV. Audiences responded positively, however, and despite initial concerns over the multi-ethnic couple, the show garnered success. *I Love Lucy* never really played Ricky's ethnicity for laughs, except to continually poke fun at his mispronunciations of American English.

LUCRATIVE DOMESTICITY

The biggest cause of the Lucy phenomenon was most likely the cultural emphasis on 1950s domesticity. *I Love Lucy* revolved around the contradictions of middle-class life, gender, marriage and the battle of the sexes, which were the concerns of television consumers and viewers. In *The "I Love Lucy" Book* by Bart Andrews, Ball remarked that the appeal of the series was

Funny Ladies

With successful comediennes such as Tina Fey, Amy Schumer, Chelsea Handler, Amy Poehler, Kristen Wiig and Ellen DeGeneres not only making people laugh as performers but also taking creative charge of comedy as writers and producers, maybe the old sexist saying that "women can't be funny" has finally been proven to be a myth. When Lucille Ball forged her career, though, strong ideas about what was funny and what was feminine shaped her choices and comedy.

"Beauty into Buffoon," the title of a Feb. 18, 1952, *Life* magazine article gets to the heart of the matter: glamorous Ball, who had been a Goldwyn showgirl and movie star, is willing to look ugly, move gracelessly and take a pie in her "fine face" for comedy.

In her book *Pretty/Funny: Women Comedians and Body Politics*, scholar Linda Mizejewski writes, "In the historic binary of 'pretty' versus 'funny,' women comics, no matter what they look like, have been located in opposition to 'pretty,' enabling them to engage in a transgressive comedy grounded in the female body — its looks, its race and sexuality, and its relationships to ideal versions of femininity. In this strand of comedy, 'pretty' is the topic and target, the ideal that is exposed as funny."

We can see this in the *I Love Lucy* episode "The Ballet," when Lucy dresses up as a ballerina, the ultimate feminine performance type. Although Lucy can wear the tutu, she can't conform to the ideal of "pretty," and Lucille Ball's performance skewers the ideal with how she uses her dancer's body to contradict what we expect from its appearance.

As the ballet teacher counts out the exercise, Lucy's body latches onto the rhythm, and Lucy's face changes to certainty instead of apprehension. She launches into the Charleston, smiling as her knees knock and legs fling in front and behind. She disrupts the ideal feminine performance of ballet with her jazzy dance moves, making fun of the feminine ideal.

Interestingly, if you look carefully at the painting on the wall above Lucy's bed in the Ricardo bedroom, you can see that it shows a ballerina. In more ways than one, ideals of femininity hang over the character's head.

Tina Fey

Amy Poehler

Ellen DeGeneres

based on "identification with millions of people. ... People identified with the Ricardos because we had the same problems they had. ... People could identify with those basic things — babysitters, traveling, wanting to be entertained, wanting to be loved in a certain way — the two couples on the show were constantly doing things that people all over the country were doing. We just took ordinary situations and exaggerated them."

Perhaps the peak of the *I Love Lucy* phenomenon was when the actors' on-screen and off-screen lives intersected when both the Ball-Arnaz and Ricardo babies were born. In fact, Desi Arnaz Jr. was born on the night that "Lucy Goes to the Hospital" aired – Jan. 19, 1953. A whopping 44 million people watched the episode in which Little Ricky was born.

Soon after that, Ball and Arnaz signed the then-

One of the show's early sponsors was Philip Morris.

Television in the 1950s

When *I Love Lucy* debuted in 1951, television was, if not in its infancy, in its toddler years. Television had been invented decades earlier, in 1928, with Philo Farnsworth making and demonstrating a working model of an electronic television in San Francisco. By 1936, RCA, which owned NBC, had a lock on producing television sets and began broadcasting live from Radio City Music Hall. There was a pause in television's spread during World War II, when the government didn't allow for the production of consumer electronics.

After World War II, television flourished. In 1946, there were only 8,000 television sets in use in the United States. By 1951 when *I Love Lucy* premiered, there were 12 million television sets. By 1954, television sets were in half of American homes, and by 1960, only 13 percent of American homes didn't have televisions.

Color televisions went on the market in 1954, but in 1957, only 150,000 color television sets had been sold. It wasn't until the mid-1960s, when the prices of color television sets dropped, picture quality improved and there were more programs in color that sales increased. By 1970, more color television sets were sold than black and white.

largest contract ever written for a television series for $8 million with the cigarette manufacturer Philip Morris and CBS. *I Love Lucy* was so valuable to its sponsor because it created a web of associations that consumers could connect to their product.

It was not only the sponsor's products that were connected to *I Love Lucy* but also a proliferation of merchandising that, in conjunction with the babies born in early 1953, surpassed $50 million. Fans could purchase *I Love Lucy* clothing for men and women, nursery sets, jewelry, comic books, record albums, dolls, aprons, his and hers pajamas and desk sets. There was even a living room furniture set exactly like the one on the show.

A 1953 magazine ad for a bedroom suite urged consumers to "Live Like Lucy!" by buying the furniture featured in the television show and also "chosen for their Hollywood home, too." This particular ad works on many levels: with associations to both the television characters and the stars, as an ad for *I Love Lucy*, and also as an ad for the matching pajamas. Blurring the line between the characters and the actors was common in magazine articles and advertisements, and it became part of the domestic story fans loved. The show made comedy out of the contradictions of consumerism and the line between "reel" and "real" life.

LUCY'S BIG BREAK

Plots frequently involved Lucy trying to get what she didn't have, and her unquenchable desire was one of her essential characteristics. When famous star Lucille Ball played starstruck Lucy — especially in the episodes set in Hollywood, where she interacted with popular actors such as John Wayne, William Holden, Harpo Marx and Rock Hudson — she mirrored the public fascination with and idolization of movie stars. When Lucy tried to go outside her role as an ordinary woman and housewife, however, she usually met with failure.

We can view Lucy's bungled efforts at paid labor as a way of portraying both men's and women's anxieties about women's increased participation in the workforce. Although we often think that women in America worked outside the home during World War II and then returned to the home when their men came back from the war, that is not completely accurate.

Despite Lucy's desire to fit certain feminine ideals, she ends up overturning these conventions with her comical hijinks.

There were more working women in 1952 than there were during the war. They didn't do the manufacturing jobs they held during the war, and many worked part-time, but the idea that 1950s women didn't work outside the home is incorrect.

Of course, the assumption that married women should not have jobs is class-based; many working-class women have always worked regardless of marital status. One of the competing cultural ideals in the series is that Lucy would not work outside the home, depend on Ricky economically and take responsibility

LIVE LIKE LUCY

(You'll Love it!)

NOW . . . FOR YOUR HOME,
THE LOVELY "I LOVE LUCY" SUITE!

Fashion Trend
By JOHNSON-CARPER

Here's The Beautiful Fashion Trend Bedroom Suite Created Especially For Lucy and Desi And Their Sensational Television Show, "I Love Lucy" — Chosen For Their Hollywood Home, Too! Brought To You By Thousands of Fashion Trend Dealers From Coast to Coast!

Double Dresser and $198.00
Bookcase Bed . . .

JOHNSON-CARPER FURNITURE CO., Inc., ROANOKE, VIRGINIA

Traditional male and female roles are depicted in the masculine and feminine dancers hanging over Lucy's and Ricky's beds (above). In-show product placement helped to sell the Ricardos' lives to millions of viewers.

for the home. However, the series also depicted the point of view that women should have careers after marriage, which was emergent in the 1950s but not yet mainstream.

This was portrayed not only by Lucy's attempts to work outside the home but also by Ball's involvement in the public sphere as an actress and a star and, most significantly, a pregnant one and then a mother. Ball, Arnaz and the writers — including Madelyn Pugh, one of the few female television writers of the time — based their work on their own understandings of gender.

WAS LUCY A FEMINIST?

When we see Lucy chafing at the confines of her role as a housewife, with everyone around her belittling her ambitions and desires beyond the home, we can see Lucy's discontent as a

> *In the pilot, Ricky says, "I want a wife who is just a wife. All you have to do is clean the house, bring me my slippers when I come home at night, cook for me, and be the mama for my children."*

precursor to the women's movement that began in the 1960s and spread during the 1970s. Lucy embodied the "feminine mystique," to use Betty Friedan's term for the postwar representation of women as both powerful and ineffective.

The writers, producers and actors on *I Love Lucy*, though, were not engaged in making a feminist show in the way that the people involved in the 1980s to '90s TV show *Murphy Brown* were. They didn't raise social issues like *All in the Family* or *Maude*, nor were they even capable of having a character aligned with women's liberation in the way that *The Mary Tyler Moore Show* did with Phyllis.

All of this is because of the time in which *I Love Lucy* was made. In the pilot, Ricky says, "I want a wife who is just a wife. All you have to do is clean the house, bring me my slippers when I come home at night, cook for me, and be the mama for my children."

I Love Lucy writer Madelyn Pugh commented in *The "I Love Lucy" Book* on this speech: "Why she didn't brain him with those slippers, I'll never know. *Mea culpa*! But it was 1951, and Lucy and I didn't know any better." What they knew was shaped by the ideas about gender and marriage of the time, and everyone involved in making *I Love Lucy* experienced a growing gap between ideas about women staying in the home and the reality of women participating in the world outside the home.

Lucy brings together the culture's contradictory ideas about women, both conveying and making fun of the concept that women want to do something beyond domestic life. *I Love Lucy* hedges its bets by making Lucy a terrible singer, so it is not only Ricky's wanting his wife to be "just a wife" — as he says in the pilot — that keeps Lucy out of the show. In the middle of any given episode, Lucy does pretty much what she wants. However, by the end, both she and Ricky are saying that they "are

even" or she has given up on her failed plan, after we have enjoyed the comic results of her attempt.

So is Lucy a feminist? Not in the way we would define the word now, as someone who advocates for women's legal, economic and social equality. However, Lucy Ricardo exhibits a proto-feminist impulse in her insistence that she is a person who is not only defined by her role as a housewife, but that she is and can be something more. Her rejection of her husband's authority over her is a move toward autonomy, which became a focus during the women's movement in the 1960s and 1970s.

Lucy's attempts to get into show biz (shown with guest star Orson Welles above) demonstrate her dissatisfaction with traditional gender roles.

When asked about the women's liberation movement in the 1970s, Lucille Ball replied, "Women's lib? It doesn't interest me one bit. I've been so liberated it hurts."

THE POWER OF COMEDY

Comedy can free people from ways of thinking that tie them to, for example, sexist ideas about gender that limit them. Comedy can also be conciliatory, so that instead of making changes in life or society, people laugh, release pent-up feelings and carry on. There are emancipatory and conciliatory aspects to the comedy in *I Love Lucy*. Did Lucy's desire to be

Lucy protests Ricky's attitudes, highlighting the growing feminist trend.

recognized as a person with talent and value make people of that time period bolder in their own lives? Did Lucy's rejection of being "just a wife" encourage female viewers to try to gain some autonomy in small or larger ways? It's hard to judge. Or was the show seen as a weekly escape to vent frustration, but then ultimately contain the audience in domesticity?

When asked about the women's liberation movement in the 1970s, Lucille Ball replied, "Women's lib? It doesn't interest me one bit. I've been so liberated it hurts." Lucille Ball had earned her own living from a young age, and as a successful actress and then the first female head of a television production studio, she'd been in positions of power and authority. Her achievements in an era without a mass women's movement were hard-won and painful.

Because of Ball's groundbreaking career both on screen and behind the scene, later comediennes — Lily Tomlin, Gilda Radner, Whoopi Goldberg, Amy Poehler and Tina Fey — have been able to use comedy to make feminist statements. They could do that because Ball unequivocally claimed comedy as women's turf and showed that women's experiences could be expressed through fearless physical comedy that didn't back away because it might be construed as unfeminine. By embodying Lucy's frustrated ambitions and recurring incompetence, Ball achieved her own ambitions, demonstrated her competence and paved the way for women to create characters that did not have to play into sexist ideas of what women were capable of.

But even more interesting than whether Lucy or Lucille Ball were feminists is how Lucy functions in how we remember the past. When we watch *I Love Lucy* today, it gives us a suitable lead-up to the mass women's movement of the 1960s and 1970s. The scholar George Lipsitz uses the term "memory as misappropriation" to describe how a television show can

Harry Ackerman, vice president of CBS-TV (top left), and Harry W. Chesley Jr., vice president of Philip Morris Co., watch as Ball and Arnaz sign a three-year, $8 million contract for *I Love Lucy* in 1953, which was the most lucrative television deal to date.

remain popular because it represents the past in a way that audiences wished it had been.

In *I Love Lucy*, the constrictions of 1950s domestic life are shown as something that Lucy can overcome through optimism, individualism and perseverance. It is easier to remember the 1950s in this simplified manner instead of grappling with a complex time that was not necessarily very fun or funny for women.

We continue to love Lucy first and foremost because she is funny. Ball's comedic performances not only stand the test of time but show a performer whose physical comedy is among the best ever captured on film. Lucy's

legacy is that *I Love Lucy* helps us make sense of the changes — and similarities — we can see in gender roles since the 1950s. It preserves a nostalgic continuum for topics that continue to command our attention in American culture, including consumerism, celebrities and what we want our home life to be. 📺

Lori Landay is Professor of Cultural Studies at Berklee College of Music. Her publications include two books: I Love Lucy *and* Madcaps, Screwballs, and Con Women: The Female Trickster in American Culture. *She has written articles about digital media, silent film and television. Her favorite episode is "The Handcuffs" (Season 2, Episode 4).*

L.A. AT LAST!

SEASON: 4
EPISODE: 16
ORIGINAL AIR DATE: Feb. 7, 1955

PLOT

The gang finally makes it to Hollywood after a long, memorable cross-country car trip. Of course Lucy's first thought is to hunt down some celebrities, and with Ricky called away to the movie studio, she decides to go to the Brown Derby with the Mertzes.

Soon, William Holden sits down in the booth directly behind Lucy, and she can't contain herself. Lucy can't stop staring, and when Holden catches her, he decides to give her a taste of her own medicine.

With Holden staring at her, Lucy nervously eats her food, but can't stand it and gets up to bolt out of the Derby and sideswipes a waiter who is holding — what else? — a tray of pies, which he drops on Holden.

Later, Ricky runs into (a now cleaned-up) Holden at the movie studio. Holden offers Ricky a ride back to his hotel, and Ricky asks him to meet his wife. When Lucy hears that Holden is in their living room, she panics and says she needs time to fix her face first.

When Lucy finally appears, she's disguised herself with a headscarf, glasses and a long false nose. Ricky is shocked, and Holden seems surprised, but they sit down for cordial conversation. Lucy's nose keeps itching, though, and when she scratches, it goes the wrong way, with Ricky and Holden staring in shock.

To deflect attention from her nose, Lucy offers Holden a cigarette and takes one herself. But when Holden goes to light her cigarette for her, her false nose catches fire. After dunking it in her coffee, Lucy finally reveals who she is.

In the first on-camera guest star appearance, Ethel asks a woman sitting at the next booth if a picture on the wall is Shelley Winters or Judy Holliday. The woman turns, revealing herself to be Eve Arden, and says, "Neither, that's Eve Arden." Arden appeared in the episode because she was shooting the show *Our Miss Brooks*, which was produced by Desilu Productions.

"Oh, Ricky, look! Hollywood's out there!"
— Lucy, upon seeing the view from their suite at the Beverly Palms Hotel for the first time

The studio making the movie *Don Juan* that Ricky is going to star in is MGM. They picked that studio because Ball and Arnaz had a relationship with MGM during their film careers.

Trivia

- William Holden had just finished shooting *The Country Girl* with Bing Crosby and Grace Kelly in real life, and he refers to this in the episode.

- After this episode, every celebrity appearing on the show asks about the Holden pie incident and is either afraid to meet Lucy or wants to know if it's true.

IN PALM SPRINGS

SEASON: 4
EPISODE: 26
ORIGINAL AIR DATE: April 25, 1955

PLOT

While in Hollywood with the Mertzes, Ricky and Lucy bicker about each other's annoying habits. Lucy hates it when Ricky taps his fingers, and the way that Lucy stirs her coffee drives Ricky crazy. Then the Mertzes start arguing, too. Fred says Ethel makes too much noise while she eats, and Ethel can't stand it when Fred jingles the keys in his pocket.

Realizing they've been spending too much time together, the group suggests splitting up. Lucy and Ethel go to Palm Springs, and Ricky and Fred stay in Hollywood.

But it's raining in Palm Springs, and the women are stuck indoors. Soon they're getting on each other's nerves with the same annoying habits that they argued about with their husbands. Back in Hollywood, Ricky and Fred bicker, too.

It dawns on the four of them that they miss their spouses, but no one wants to admit they were wrong. Then Ricky gets a call asking him to come to Palm Springs to meet with a studio bigwig, and off go he and Fred.

It's stopped raining in Palm Springs, and Lucy and Ethel are by the pool when actor Rock Hudson introduces himself to Lucy and asks if he can share a story with her. A woman named Adele Sliff's husband had an annoying whistling habit. Eventually the woman got so fed up with the whistling that she left him. Later, on his way to make up with his wife, the whistling husband had an accident, and his wife begs him to whistle one last time, but he can't.

Lucy and Ethel are touched by the story and thrilled when their husbands appear at the pool. The men laugh and admit that the story about the whistling husband wasn't true; they made it up to soften their wives toward them. Then Lucy confesses that she pretended to be the secretary of the studio head to trick Ricky into coming to Palm Springs. Lucy tells Hudson he must think they're crazy, and he agrees with her: They *are* crazy!

"Would you like a piece of rock, Mr. Candy?"

— Ethel, upon meeting Rock Hudson

Lucy tries to trick Ricky with the coin toss, saying, "Heads, we go. Tails, you stay." Ricky doesn't fall for it, though, as she apparently pulled the same trick to get him to marry her.

Trivia

- The gang's annoying habits are supposedly habitual, but they're never again mentioned in the series.

- The story Rock Hudson tells is about a woman named Adele Sliff, the name of *I Love Lucy*'s script supervisor.

PRODUCING
Lucy

Desi and Lucy changed the TV industry forever when they formed their own company named Desilu.

BY ERIC HILLIS

In 2015, actor Leonard Nimoy passed away at age 83. Though he enjoyed a varied career, Nimoy will forever be associated with his role as *Star Trek*'s Spock, arguably one of the most recognizable TV characters. Both the character and the show preached tolerance and multiculturalism, but the production company that made *Star Trek* possible, Desilu Productions, was founded by a married couple out of necessity, prompted by an instance of intolerance.

HOW IT ALL BEGAN

Since 1948, Lucille Ball had appeared on the hit CBS radio show *My Favorite Husband* as Liz Cugat, with actor Richard Denning (best known for his roles in 1950s science-fiction movies) playing her "favorite" husband, George. After 20 episodes, the fictional couple's Latin surname, Cugat, was dropped for the more Anglo-Saxon Cooper — ironic because Ball was married to a Cuban immigrant, Desi Arnaz.

Desilu Productions owned three separate studios, including the Gower location (with its distinctive water tower, opposite page) and the Culver City studio where *Gone with the Wind* was filmed.

My Favorite Husband, a radio show that inspired *I Love Lucy*, was brought to television in 1953 (above) — but without the same success as *I Love Lucy*. The pilot episode of *I Love Lucy* was filmed on March 2, 1951. In it, Lucy plays a clown during Ricky's audition for a TV show (left).

With the radio show attracting a large audience, CBS was keen to adapt it for the then-growing medium of television. Ball agreed to the switch on the condition that Arnaz would replace Denning as her on-screen husband. CBS executives initially balked at the idea, but Ball and Arnaz won them over.

Subsequently, Ball and Arnaz founded their own production company, blending their first names to form Desilu, with Arnaz acting as president and Ball as vice-president. Using their own finances, they produced a pilot for a show that would later become *I Love Lucy*. Thanks to the formation of Desilu and the popularity of their act, Ball and Arnaz held all the cards.

Desilu began renting space at General Service Studios in Hollywood. They used Stage Two, which was named Desilu Playhouse.

RAPID EXPANSION

Of course, what happened next is the stuff of TV legend. The show became a sensation soon after it first aired, with Ball and Arnaz at the center of production. Because they had negotiated to retain all rights to the show, Desilu held a valuable commodity and was in a strong position financially. Essentially, Ball and Arnaz created the concept of the rerun with their deft negotiating to retain the rights to *I Love Lucy*.

The success of *I Love Lucy* was only the beginning for Desilu. At the time, it was the only independent production company in television, and the studio began to produce other shows, beginning with *Our Miss Brooks* during the 1952 to 1953 season. While Arnaz took care of the business side of the company, Ball made the creative choices, seeking out shows that combined commercial appeal with her own progressive values.

Like *I Love Lucy*, *Our Miss Brooks* began as a hit CBS radio show. Eve Arden played the title role of Connie Brooks, a high school English teacher. Such strong, self-determined female characters were a rarity on TV in the early 1950s, and Brooks reflected the proto-feminist outlook of Lucille Ball. Brooks was a go-getter, particularly when it came to pursuing her male love interest, Philip Boynton, played by Robert Rockwell. At a time when single women were expected to wait around for a marriage proposal, portraying Brooks as she actively chased the clueless Boynton was progressive and hilarious to viewers.

In 1953 and 1954, Desilu began to take advantage of its innovative setup by filming shows for other production companies, including *The Jack Benny Program* for J&M Productions and Marterto Productions' *Make Room for Daddy*.

With the company rapidly expanding, it was time to leave General Service Studios. In 1954, Desilu purchased its own studio, the Motion Picture Center at Hollywood's Cahuenga Boulevard, renaming the facility Desilu Cahuenga Studios. At the time, it was the only studio in Hollywood capable of accommodating live audiences.

By the 1956 to 1957 season, Desilu was producing six of its own shows while renting space and filming shows for a host of other production companies. Desilu needed more room to keep up with the company's rapid expansion. Luckily, as Ball and Arnaz had retained the rights to *I Love Lucy*, they had a gold mine they could tap to fund their necessary investments: the syndication rights for the show. After selling the rights to the first 180 episodes back to CBS in 1957 for nearly $5 million, Desilu purchased the production facilities of RKO Pictures (then owned by the General Tire and Rubber Company) for around $6 million. This added two new facilities to Desilu: the former RKO facility at Gower Street in Hollywood — renamed Desilu Gower — and the former RKO-Pathé lot in Culver City — renamed Desilu Culver.

Desi Arnaz had a cameo as himself in an episode of *Our Miss Brooks*.

THE TOP INDEPENDENT

For the next 10 years, Desilu could boast that it was the only production company to operate three separate studios. Covering a combined total area of 63 acres, Desilu had more than 30 soundstages and over 500 offices spread across its three facilities. Desilu Gower, where a distinctive water tower bore the inscription "Desilu Studios," became the company's headquarters and was home to New York Street, a weatherproof mock-up of a typical East Coast city street. Desilu Culver housed a facility known as 40 Acres, home to sets like Chicago Street, Suburban Street and Western Street. It also boasted Hollywood's largest soundstage among its 13 stages.

In the 1958 to 1959 season, Desilu added to its lineup a new show titled *Westinghouse*

Desilu Playhouse. The hour-long show utilized an anthology format with a distinct story told each week, and several episodes featured Arnaz and Ball in roles different from those they had become famous for on *I Love Lucy*. Westinghouse Electric paid an unprecedented $12 million to sponsor the show, and in one of the earliest examples of product placement, the company's products were integrated into the show's sets.

On Nov. 24, 1958, an episode titled "The Time Element" aired. A science-fiction tale incorporating time travel and the attack on Pearl Harbor, "The Time Element" was penned by a writer named Rod Serling, who initially wrote it as a pilot for a proposed sci-fi anthology. CBS had purchased the script but later declined to adapt it. Then the producer of *Westinghouse*

Desilu at the Movies

Though Lucille Ball and Desi Arnaz were powerhouses in the television industry, their attempts to produce motion pictures met with disaster.

Their first film, *Forever, Darling* (1956; pictured top right), was a romantic comedy starring Arnaz and Ball, who hoped to replicate the success of *The Long, Long Trailer*, which was released in 1954 by MGM. In *Forever, Darling*, Arnaz is a neglectful spouse, and Ball is his unhappy wife whose guardian angel advises her to take a greater interest in his work. Arnaz felt the script was weak and brought in *I Love Lucy* writers Madelyn Pugh and Bob Carroll Jr. to salvage it. The results were less than stellar.

The movie didn't do well at the box office, barely returning its production cost of $1.4 million. The failure prompted MGM to opt out of its two-picture deal with Desilu, and Arnaz decided to drop plans for a feature-film division at the company.

Desilu wouldn't attempt to enter the world of film production again until 1967, with the release of *Yours, Mine and Ours* (pictured bottom right), starring Ball, Henry Fonda and Van Johnson. The movie was both a critical and financial success. It was Desilu's last attempt. By the time of the movie's release, Ball had sold her interest in Desilu.

Desilu Playhouse, Bert Granet, came across the script and greenlighted its production. The episode was a hit with audiences and critics, and CBS, realizing they had been too hasty in dismissing Serling, agreed to produce his proposed show. "The Time Element" served as a backdoor pilot for one of TV's most iconic science-fiction shows: *The Twilight Zone*.

April 20, 1959, saw the airing of the first part of *Westinghouse Desilu Playhouse*'s first and only two-part story. *The Untouchables* starred Robert Stack as the real-life U.S. Department of the Treasury agent Eliot Ness and was adapted by writer Paul Monash from Ness' 1947 memoir. Based on Ness' battle with infamous mobster Al Capone, *The Untouchables* was so popular with viewers that it, too, served as an unofficial pilot for an iconic series. Desilu pitched the series to CBS, which declined, before NBC purchased the show.

WOMAN IN POWER

In 1962, with the couple now divorced for two years, Ball bought out her ex-husband's share in the company, taking over as president of Desilu. In doing so, she became the first female head of a major Hollywood studio, arguably making her the most powerful woman in the industry. Ball ran Desilu until 1967, when she sold the company to Gulf & Western Industries, owners of Paramount Pictures, which renamed it Paramount Television. In her final year as head of Desilu, Ball helped launch two of television's most iconic shows.

In 1966, spies and secret agents were everywhere in movies and TV. The success of the James Bond movies led to hugely popular small-screen shows like *The Man from U.N.C.L.E.* and *The Avengers*. When writer Bruce Geller approached Desilu with the concept for *Mission: Impossible*, Ball was sure she had a winner on her hands. CBS didn't see it that way and refused to adapt Geller's idea. Ball went ahead and produced a pilot anyway. The resulting show would run for the next seven years, inspiring a 1988 revival and a big-screen franchise starring Tom Cruise.

Ball made her biggest off-screen contribution to television and pop culture when she agreed to produce a pilot for a sci-fi show created by a former cop-turned-TV-writer named Gene Roddenberry. The show was *Star Trek*, a series

Like *I Love Lucy*, *The Untouchables* had its own controversies, including a lawsuit by the Capone family for its depiction in the series.

that aimed to tackle science fiction in a serious manner, using the format to comment indirectly on contemporary issues. Ball's advisors warned her it would be expensive to produce and limited in its appeal. But the show's progressive message appealed to Ball. Again she took a chance and produced a pilot, and TV's biggest franchise was born.

When Paramount bought Desilu, they acquired two properties in *Mission: Impossible* and *Star Trek* that would become the jewels in the studio's crown. A fifth *Mission: Impossible* movie is coming to theaters in 2015, with a 13th *Star Trek* film scheduled for 2016. Neither will bear the Desilu logo, but they wouldn't exist without Lucille Ball. ▢

Eric Hillis is a freelance writer from Dublin who writes about cinema and TV for a variety of publications and websites including his own site, themoviewaffler.com. His natural habitat is the darkened screening rooms in Dublin, where he spends most mornings with fellow film critics.

HARPO MARX

SEASON: 4
EPISODE: 28
ORIGINAL AIR DATE: May 9, 1955

At the end of the episode, Ricky dressed as Groucho and Fred disguised as Chico arrive ' to meet (and trick) Carolyn Appleby, but it's too late, she's already left.

PLOT

Lucy's friend Carolyn Appleby plans to stop in Hollywood for a visit on her way to Hawaii, and she expects to meet a lot of movie stars because Lucy has been telling tall tales in her letters back home. Lucy panics, then comes up with a scheme: Steal Carolyn's glasses. Without them, Carolyn is so near-sighted she won't be able to recognize Lucy when she disguises herself as different celebrities.

One by one, Lucy comes in wearing masks of different celebrities — Gary Cooper, Clark Gable and Jimmy Durante. Ethel manages to keep Carolyn just far enough away so she believes that she's actually meeting movie stars.

Little does Lucy know that while they're at the pool, Ricky and Fred have bumped into Harpo Marx, who is staying at the hotel for a woman's club benefit, and they ask him go upstairs and see Lucy and meet her friend.

Harpo comes in and, after a quick intro, leaves to retrieve his harp. While he is gone, Carolyn goes to the restroom and Lucy enters, dressed as Harpo. Ethel tells her that the real Harpo is on his way, so Lucy hides.

Harpo plays "Take Me Out to the Ball Game" for Ethel and Carolyn. When Carolyn has to leave, Harpo throws her over his shoulder and carries her out.

When Harpo returns, he spies Lucy in the kitchen. Then, in a scene reminiscent of the Marx Brothers' movie *Duck Soup* (1933), Harpo and Lucy do the "mirror" scene where Lucy perfectly mimics all of Harpo's movements and facial expressions. She is exposed when they both take off their hats and drop them, but Harpo's hat bounces back up, while Lucy's falls to the ground.

> *"Ricky, I'm not asking for much.*
> *All I want is half a dozen movie stars*
> *for a couple of hours."*

— Lucy, when she finds out that Carolyn Appleby
is coming to Hollywood to visit her

Trivia

• Lucy was in the 1938 movie *Room Service* with the Marx brothers.

• Harpo had a heart attack shortly before this episode. His doctor advised him not to do the show, but Harpo insisted. While he had fun working with the *I Love Lucy* cast and crew, Harpo had another heart attack soon after he filmed the episode.

LUCY'S ITALIAN MOVIE

SEASON: 5
EPISODE: 23
ORIGINAL AIR DATE: April 16, 1956

PLOT

On a cramped train headed toward Rome, the Ricardos and Mertzes struggle to get comfortable, and Lucy complains to Ricky that she's being ogled by a "typical masher" (meaning, someone who pays unwanted attention to a woman). When the foursome wakes up the next morning, the man approaches their train car, and Ricky confronts him.

He turns out to be Vittorio Felipe, an Italian movie producer who offers Lucy a role in his new movie titled *Bitter Grapes*. Lucy assumes her part will involve something to do with winemaking. She says she wants to learn about Italian winemaking to prepare for her role, but Ricky warns her not to go about "soaking up local color."

While the men are away, Lucy ignores Ricky's advice and finds a local winery in a small town named Turo that still does things the old-fashioned way — meaning, pressing grapes by foot. When a man comes to assign jobs for the day, Lucy is picked to stomp grapes, because her feet are like "large pizzas." She proceeds to mimic the other vat worker, Teresa, an older, short Italian woman, and climbs into the grape vat.

Though at first Lucy doesn't like the feeling of the grapes on her feet, she quickly gets into it and begins stomping around the vat. Before too long, though, she's pooped out and tries to quit. Teresa insists that Lucy get back to work. A comic brawl ensues, and Lucy ends up wrestling with the feisty Italian woman in the vat.

Back at their hotel, Ricky is waiting with Felipe to speak with Lucy. When Felipe sees her covered in grape stains, he explains that she's completely misunderstood him, and that the movie has nothing to do with winemaking. He regretfully informs Lucy that she can't be in the picture, because he can't take the chance she won't be back to normal the following morning. Lucy's extremely upset, especially when Felipe notices Ethel and offers her the part instead.

Lucille Ball didn't practice with real grapes until filming the scene, wanting her reaction to be authentic. She said mashing the grapes felt like "stepping on eyeballs."

"Boy, when it comes to soakin' up local color, you don't mess around!"
— Fred, upon seeing Lucy's grape-stained appearance

Trivia

- The Italian version of the movie title is *Grappolo Pungente*, meaning pungent grapes.

- Teresa, the woman in the vat with Lucy, was a real grape-stomper from Napa Valley.

- The Ricardos and Mertzes had to endure an overnight 13-hour train ride from Florence to Rome, but the trip actually only takes about an hour and a half.

GROUNDBREAKING
Lucy

*Live audiences, three cameras, televised pregnancy and interracial marriage —
I Love Lucy was at the forefront of making cultural and television history.*

BY GILLIAN G. GAAR

Since the first episode of *I Love Lucy* debuted on Oct. 15, 1951, the show has never been off the air. Following the original run of 181 episodes and the 13 one-hour specials that aired between 1957 and 1960 as *The Lucille Ball-Desi Arnaz Show* — later modified to *The Lucy–Desi Comedy Hour* — the show has lived on in syndication. According to *TV Guide*, 40 million Americans still watch the show in reruns — an especially impressive figure considering the program has been available on VHS and DVD (and now Blu-ray) for years. And it regularly features prominently on "Best TV Series of All Time" lists.

There are good reasons for the show's longevity. The quality of the scripts and Lucille Ball's skill in physical comedy are major factors that keep people watching the episodes again and again. But there are other elements that played a part in creating a show that was built to last.

Through its six-season run, *I Love Lucy* broke new ground and reinvented the business of television, creating a lasting masterpiece for fans.

INTERRACIAL COUPLE

I Love Lucy's roots go back to the CBS radio series *My Favorite Husband*. The series, which ran from 1948 to 1951, starred Richard Denning and Lucille Ball as a husband and wife who live in the fictional city of Sheridan Falls. The show was a success, and in 1950, CBS decided to move the program to television. The original plan was to have Denning and Ball reprise their roles, but Ball had a different objective.

She wanted the husband's role to be played by her real-life husband, bandleader Desi Arnaz. Over the years, their career paths had led to their living separate lives. "We had been married 10 years," Arnaz said. "Yet we were almost total strangers. Our work pulled us far apart, East Coast and West." Working on the same show would give the couple the chance to be together.

CBS was opposed for a reason that seems archaic today — the Arnaz-Ball relationship was interracial. The network was also concerned that Arnaz's accent was too thick to be easily understood and that, as a bandleader, he didn't have the acting chops. There were also concerns that no one would believe that the wholesome, all-American Lucille Ball could possibly be married to a Cuban. The couple dismissed that notion as ridiculous; after all, they were married in real life, weren't they?

The two were determined to prove that the public would accept them, and they decided to create an act to take on the road. Two of *My Favorite Husband*'s writers, Bob Carroll Jr. and Madelyn Pugh, were engaged to write comedy material for a show billed as "Desi Arnaz & Band with Lucille Ball." The act toured the country to a good reception, and CBS finally agreed to cast Arnaz in the new show. Thus *I Love Lucy* had broken one barrier before a single scene had even been filmed.

The show's pilot was shot in March 1951; Carroll and Pugh were brought in as writers along with *My Favorite Husband*'s head writer, Jess Oppenheimer, who also became the show's producer and chose the program's title, picking *I Love Lucy* because he felt it conveyed "the essential nature of the

It was considered risqué to depict Lucille Ball and Desi Arnaz as a married couple in 1951.

Lighting and Editing Challenges

Recording on film posed its own challenges, mainly because of the difficulty of lighting a stage. To complicate things even more, Desi Arnaz came up with the idea of shooting simultaneously with three cameras — in front of a live studio audience no less. This would allow them to capture wide, medium and close-up shots, but it presented unique problems for cameramen.

On film shoots, lighting was rearranged between takes to capture different angles, but this would be impossible for a show recorded in a single take. Cameramen from the TV industry were stumped, so Desilu looked to the world of movies and recruited one of the most revered cinematographers in Hollywood.

Karl Freund began his career in Germany, where he photographed classics of silent cinema such as *Metropolis*, *The Golem* and *The Last Laugh*. He then made the move to Hollywood and established the visual template for Universal Studios' horror movies with his work on 1931's *Dracula*. He worked with Lucille Ball on the 1943 musical comedy *Du Barry Was a Lady*, and they reunited in 1945's *Without Love*.

Karl Freund's idea to light everything from above soon became the industry standard for TV Shows.

Freund clearly impressed the actress, and in 1951, she approached the cinematographer with Desilu's conundrum. Freund initially dismissed the notion of shooting with three cameras, claiming it was impossible. Arnaz and Ball refused to take no for an answer, however, and Freund accepted the challenge.

Freund's solution was to light the set from above, flooding every part of the stage to remove the shadows. Known as "flat lighting," this technique soon became the standard practice for shooting before a live studio audience and remains common for sitcoms today.

Shooting with three cameras also created extra work for the show's editors, Dean Cahn and his assistant, Bud Molin. This led to another piece of innovation on Desilu's part. At the time, TV shows were edited using a Moviola, which only allowed for the editing of footage from two cameras at a time. This made cutting an episode of *I Love Lucy* a lengthy and extremely challenging process.

Cahn and Molin were editing three 30-minute episodes a week and badly needed a more efficient solution. They worked with Mark Serrurier Jr., whose father Iwan was the creator of the original Moviola, and developed a new machine capable of editing three reels of film along with a soundtrack reel. The "three-headed monster," as it was called, quickly became the industry standard.

To accommodate a live audience and the extra camera equipment required, Desilu needed its own studio. General Service Studios was a seven-and-a-half acre Hollywood facility housing eight soundstages. Desilu rented its Stage Two and renamed it Desilu Playhouse. The stage was renovated extensively to house the bleachers for the live audience and to make room for the movement of three cameras. — *Eric Hillis*

Ball with cameraman Karl Freund on *Du Barry Was a Lady* (1943).

show — an examination of marriage between two people who truly love each other." Cigarette company Philip Morris signed on as the show's sponsor.

EAST VS. WEST

Now there was another obstacle. Ball was expecting her first child, and the couple hoped to stay in Hollywood and raise their family there. At the time, most shows were shot on the East Coast for broadcast there and in the Midwest. A kinescope — essentially, a film of a video monitor — was made for later broadcast on the West Coast.

When Ball and Arnaz wanted to reverse the process, filming in the West then sending the show to the East Coast and Midwest, Philip Morris said no; that meant the larger markets would only be able to experience *I Love Lucy* via poorer quality kinescopes. Nor would they agree to cover the costs of shooting the show on film (filming having higher quality). Ball's agent, Don Sharpe, worked out a solution: CBS would help cover the costs of shooting on film,

while Ball and Arnaz would take a cut in their salaries. In return, the couple's company, Desilu Productions, was granted 80 percent of the film negative rights; 15 percent was given to producer/writer Oppenheimer; and the remaining 5 percent was split between Carroll and Pugh. This decision meant that *I Love Lucy* would be preserved in a higher quality format, something future generations of *Lucy* fans would be profoundly grateful for when the show began to be rerun. It was later made available for sale on VHS and DVD. Desilu Productions later sold its share of *I Love Lucy*'s film rights to CBS for the tidy sum of $5 million.

LIVE AUDIENCE

Having a live audience for a television show was unusual when *I Love Lucy* aired. Most series at the time used a laugh track. But *I Love Lucy* was designed to take advantage of Ball's skills with physical comedy, which would work better if she had an audience to play off of. Even the in-studio audiences for *My Favorite Husband* would laugh at the faces Ball pulled while reading her lines. But this also meant locating a space that could accommodate an audience.

The show eventually set up shop at General Service Studios in Hollywood, which had eight soundstages. Two of them were converted for the *I Love Lucy* team. Because the soundstages weren't being used for anything else, the production crew could build sturdier, permanent sets as opposed to sets that had to be disassembled when another show used the studio.

The production schedule for the show was tight. In the early years, a read-through of the script was held on a Monday. By Tuesday afternoon, rehearsals started. On Wednesday, rehearsals began on the set. On Thursday, the camera crew began its rehearsal on the set, followed by rehearsals with the cast and crew. A final dress rehearsal was held Friday afternoon, and the show was filmed Friday night at 8 p.m.

Great importance was put on rehearsals because the team wanted to perform the show with minimal breaks in the action. "We had stops for Lucy's big costume changes, but that was all," director William Asher told writer Ted Elrick. "I had a pretty strict rule on that.

Ball fed off the live audience's laughter, using it to judge timing for gags.

The three-camera approach used on *I Love Lucy* revolutionized television and still serves as the template for most sitcoms today.

We didn't stop for anything. We played it like a Broadway show. If an actor made a mistake or forgot a line or something like that, it was up to the other actors to get him out of it." The audience's genuine reactions made watching the show more enjoyable, and today, shooting a television show in front of a live audience is something that's taken for granted. This also led to declining use of a "laugh track," something that was phased out by the end of the 1970s.

LUCY'S "EXPECTING"

From the beginning, the writers had crafted storylines that the general public could easily relate to. But Ball's pregnancy during the show's second season pushed the program into new territory. Ball had actually been pregnant with her first child, Lucie Désirée Arnaz, when she filmed the *I Love Lucy* pilot, but no mention was made of her condition. And when Arnaz came to Oppenheimer toward the end of *I Love Lucy*'s first season and told him that Ball was again pregnant, both men assumed the show would have to go off the air, at least temporarily.

It was Oppenheimer who came up with the idea of writing Ball's pregnancy into the show. At first, CBS and Philip Morris opposed this idea. Aside from *Mary Kay and Johnny* (a sitcom starring Mary Kay and Johnny Stearns, which ran from 1947 to 1950), pregnant women weren't seen on television. But Arnaz appealed directly to the chairman of Philip Morris, and they finally agreed. CBS also agreed,

CBS agreed, but with the proviso that the word "pregnant" could not be uttered; "expecting" or "with child" were deemed acceptable. To further allay concerns, Oppenheimer arranged for a priest, a minister and a rabbi to approve the shows that dealt with the pregnancy in order to provide further assurance that there was nothing objectionable in them.

Depicting pregnancy on-camera was unheard of in the 1950s.

but with the proviso that the world "pregnant" could not be uttered; "expecting" or "with child" were deemed acceptable. To further allay concerns, Oppenheimer arranged for a priest, a minister and a rabbi to approve the shows that dealt with the pregnancy in order to provide further assurance that there was nothing in them that the general public would find objectionable.

The first show to deal with the pregnancy, "Lucy is Enceinte" (*enceinte* being the French word for "pregnant"), aired on Dec. 8, 1952. The show did receive 200 complaints from viewers about Ball's "condition," but it was a number quickly dwarfed by the 30,000 other viewers who sent in congratulations. Seven episodes dealt with the pregnancy, culminating in the birth of "Little Ricky" on "Lucy Goes to the Hospital," which aired on Jan. 19, 1953.

The episode attracted a record-breaking audience of 44 million views (over 70 percent of the television viewing audience), 15 million more people than would watch President Dwight D. Eisenhower's inauguration address the next day, as Oppenheimer gleefully noted in his autobiography called *Laughs, Lucy ... and Lucy: How I Came to Create the Most Popular Sitcom of All Time.* Ball also gave birth to her real-life son on Jan. 19, welcoming Desiderio Alberto Arnaz IV (aka Desi Arnaz Jr.) to the world. The narrative arc about Ball's "expecting" had injected an element of real life into the show — and proved to be wildly popular. Another barrier had been broken.

WHO KNEW?

One fact that's little known is that the teleprompter was invented for *I Love Lucy*. Oppenheimer created (and patented) what he called the "Jayo Viewer" in order to help Ball and Arnaz read ad copy for the show's com-

I Love Lucy was responsible for numerous firsts in television history and gave modern audiences a format that endures today.

mercials. An article in *Variety* pointed out that the invention would not only benefit news-readers but also politicians making speeches, as has indeed proven to be the case. And who would've guessed it began with *I Love Lucy*?

One of the show's biggest innovations was something that had unforeseen consequences at the time. In the fall of 1955, CBS began showing *I Love Lucy* reruns on Saturday night. To their astonishment, the reruns landed in the Top 10, getting higher ratings than some first-run shows (including *The Honeymooners*). This helped create the market for reruns and syndications, something that has allowed in-numerable TV shows to live on in perpetuity — though none have had the staying power of *I Love Lucy*.

Reruns, shooting before a live audience and the teleprompter — even if you never saw an episode of the program, *I Love Lucy* changed the way we watch television forever. ▢

Gillian G. Gaar is an entertainment writer based in Seattle. She is the author of more than 10 books and has written for national and international publications. Her favorite episode is "Lucy Does a TV Commercial" (see page 10).

LUCY AND SUPERMAN

SEASON: 6
EPISODE: 13
ORIGINAL AIR DATE: Jan. 14, 1957

PLOT

After watching *Adventures of Superman* and putting Little Ricky to bed, Lucy and Ricky have guests — the Applebys, a couple with whom the Ricardos clearly feel competitive. Carolyn Appleby's son Stevie and Little Ricky were born just four days apart. Both mothers are planning birthday parties for their sons ... on the same day. The women argue over who should reschedule the party, and both refuse.

Lucy fears that all of the children in the class will go to Stevie's party because of the clown, puppet show and magician that Carolyn has arranged. Lucy decides she must one-up the Applebys, and who better to invite than Superman? Ricky has met Superman, so Lucy asks Ricky to invite him to the party.

Ricky tries his best, but Superman can't come to the party. Having already promised Little Ricky — and Carolyn — that Superman will be there, Lucy decides to dress up as the superhero and "fly" past their apartment window. In reality, Lucy plans to use the vacant apartment next door, climb out the window and walk on the ledge past her own apartment window so the children get to see "Superman."

Little Ricky's party begins, and Lucy goes next door to put on her Superman costume. She climbs out the window, exiting the vacant apartment just as prospective tenants arrive.

Meanwhile, the actual Superman arrives! Having heard it was a child's birthday party, Superman changed his plans so he could be there. Lucy tries to go back to her apartment via the vacant apartment, but the Mertzes' prospective tenants are there, so she stays on the ledge ... just as it begins to rain. Lucy is now trapped!

The party ends, and when Ricky is told that Lucy is on the ledge outside, he goes to save her. But Lucy's cape is stuck on a drainpipe as the rain continues to fall. It's Superman to the rescue as he climbs out on the ledge to help Lucy.

"And they call me Superman!"

— Superman, upon hearing that Ricky has been married to Lucy for 15 years

The name of George Reeves, the actor who played Superman, did not appear in the script or the credits for the episode — perhaps to prevent disillusioning children who believed he was the real thing.

Trivia

• Wheels were added to the bottom of the Ricardos' piano so Superman could easily move it aside to go out on the ledge and save Lucy.

• We're told it's Little Ricky's fifth birthday, but he was born in 1953 and should have been turning 4.

LUCY GOES TO SCOTLAND

SEASON: 5
EPISODE: 17
ORIGINAL AIR DATE: Feb. 20, 1956

PLOT

In what is considered by some the worst episode of the series, Lucy wants to go to Scotland while the Ricardos and Mertzes are in Europe so she can look up her ancestors — particularly her great-great-great grandfather Angus MacGillicuddy from the town of Kildoonan. Before going to bed that night, Lucy plays with a toy dragon Fred bought for Little Ricky.

Lucy falls asleep and dreams that she's in Kildoonan and the mayor and the townspeople welcome her with fanfare and song when they find out she is a MacGillicuddy descendant. To prove that she is a MacGillicuddy, Lucy must do the "sword dance," which she completely flubs. The mayor exclaims that she is most definitely a MacGillicuddy because the family can't dance "worth a hoot." She's excited until she finds out that the town is terrorized by a two-headed dragon who must feed on a MacGillicuddy every 30 years.

Enter Scotty MacTavish MacDougal MacCardo (Ricky doing a terrible Scottish brogue), who is tasked to watch over Lucy until she is fed to the dragon. It's love at first sight for Scotty who sings "I'm in Love with a Dragon's Dinner" to Lucy.

They go off to the dragon's lair to try to talk reason with the two-headed dragon (Fred and Ethel), who keep bickering with each other, but the one thing they agree on is that they must eat a MacGillicuddy.

Scotty and Lucy return to Kildoonan, where Scotty says he will fight the dragon with his bare hands. But when the dragon comes to town, Scotty chickens out and tries to throw Lucy to the dragon.

Lucy wakes up and hits Ricky over the head with her pillow and calls him a coward.

"Lucy Goes to Scotland" is a comical take on *Brigadoon*, a musical and movie about a mysterious Scottish village that appears for one day every 100 years.

Trivia

• During one of the songs, Lucy pulls out an LP (album). Scotty looks at it and says, "Xavier MacCugat!" as a nod to Desi Arnaz's early mentor, Xavier Cugat.

• Larry Orenstein wrote all the songs for the episode and stars as the mayor; Desi said that no one could sing the songs better than Larry.

"Get a load of those drumsticks!"

— Dragon Fred, upon seeing Lucy's legs

Goodbye, Lucy

After six successful seasons, I Love Lucy *transformed into* The Lucy-Desi Comedy Hour *for three years before finally shutting down.*

BY THOMAS WAGNER

Toward the end of season 6 of *I Love Lucy*, Desi Arnaz flew to New York City to meet with Bill Paley, the founder of CBS and architect of its evolution into a media behemoth. Paley was not just the powerful president of the network; he was also regarded as the pontiff of broadcasting — respected, revered and sometimes feared.

To say that Arnaz had come to drop a bomb on his boss understates the circumstance that day by many orders of magnitude. He informed the disbelieving Paley that he and Lucille Ball wanted to terminate CBS's No. 1-rated show in its weekly half-hour format and go forward with hour-long specials to be aired once a month.

Imagining the pillar of his Monday-night schedule, indeed the anchor of CBS's success, disappearing down the drain, Paley responded, "What are you talking about? You're the number-one show on television. You can't quit now!"

WEEKLY TO MONTHLY

If Arnaz's powers of persuasion were legendary, he now pulled out all the stops to reassure his anxious boss, suggesting that after more than 150

Fred MacMurray (center) with the rest of the gang in the episode "Lucy Hunts Uranium" (1958).

Milton Berle

Red Skelton

episodes, the best way to preserve the audience's affection for the popular sitcom was to reduce how often they could see it. He implied that the pressure to maintain originality and freshness from script to script had worn down the writers. Arnaz maintained that Desilu had never produced a bad episode, and he planned to keep it that way.

Reluctantly, he also confessed his own weariness. Arnaz had been toiling on both sides of the camera for many years, maintaining high standards on his own hit show as well as dozens of others that Desilu produced. Even for a man with boundless energy and a photographic memory, it was a crushing load. It took an inevitable toll on his family life and his health.

Weighing his options, Paley decided that Lucy once a month was better than no Lucy at all.

GUEST STARS AND HIGH RATINGS

As season 6 of *I Love Lucy* progressed, the Ricardos relocated to the suburbs of Connecticut with the Mertzes in tow. Arnaz determined that his role as Ricky would recede in importance and screen time as would William Frawley's Fred. Vivian Vance, as Ethel, would still be Lucy's sidekick and partner in lunacy, but Arnaz also wanted to feature a different celebrity guest each week to generate additional star power.

And the stars appeared on cue — a caravan of Hollywood luminaries all lined up to share the fun and the spotlight with Lucy. Milton Berle, Tallulah Bankhead, Fred MacMurray, Maurice Chevalier, Ida Lupino, Danny Thomas and Red Skelton — they all took a turn opposite television's favorite redhead.

The Lucy-Desi Comedy Hour comprised 13 one-hour episodes in total, broadcast over three seasons. Ratings remained high, at least until the final season. By that time, although invisible to their fans, the Arnazes' marriage was going south in a hurry. The anguish born of 10 years of living and working together every day and the resentment and damage caused by Arnaz's infidelity erupted into bitter fights. Inevitably the strain spilled onto the set, touching everyone, cast and crew alike. There was no turning back.

LAST EPISODE, LAST SONG

The final episode, "The Mustache," was shot on March 2, 1960, with Ernie Kovacs and his wife, Edie Adams, as guest stars. Arnaz, who directed the episode, requested that Adams, a popular singer, bring a song to perform.

Years later, Adams recalled the scene vividly: "I remember choosing the song very carefully. It was a favorite of Ernie's and mine. I didn't think anything of it at the time. But when we went into rehearse, it was obvious that things were not all well with Desi and Lucy. And I thought, 'Uh-oh, we're in for a bumpy ride.'"

She wasn't kidding. The tension on the set was palpable. Communications had so completely broken down that they were no longer speaking directly to each other except as the script demanded. It was a sad and depressing ordeal for two stars who shared such an extraordinary journey and whose legacy would one day represent an indelible chapter in broadcast history.

Edie Adams chose "That's All" by Alan Brandt and Bob Haymes. The lyrics include these lines: *"I can only give you love that lasts forever / And a promise to be near each time you call / And a love whose burning light / Will warm the winter night / That's all, that's all / I love you, yes, I love you / That's all."*

Adams called it, "A poem, a poem to love ... and in my nearsighted eyes, I thought everyone was crying. And I thought, 'Oh my, what have I done; I picked this song and now everybody's crying.' I just inadvertently picked the most inappropriate song for that day."

Maury Thompson, the script supervisor, had his own heartbreaking memories: "We knew for a long time it wasn't going to work. [But] it was our family ... we were a family. We went on picnics together ... they were so strong together as lovers, we just couldn't believe that they would allow it to happen ... to all of us."

The very last scene called for them to kiss. Arnaz remembered it as a kiss that would "wrap up 20 years ... of heartbreaks and laughter." When they broke, both were crying.

Lucille spoke first: "You're supposed to say 'cut.'"

Edie Adams remembered thinking sadly, "It was the end of an era in television that I don't think we'll see again."

She was right. ▢

Thomas Wagner is an Emmy Award-winning writer and composer living in New York City.

Tallulah Bankhead

Rudy Vallee

Lucy
Ricardo

Lucille Ball • Aug. 6, 1911 – April 26, 1989

The Redhead

Lucille Ball combined her incredible work ethic and extraordinary comedic talent to become the first lady of sitcom.

BY THOMAS WAGNER

By 1948, Lucille Ball's movie career had peaked without ever reaching the top of the mountain. After appearing in close to 70 motion pictures, her grandest achievement was earning the dubious title "Queen of the B-Movies." She was a major star in the minor leagues, approaching 40 and bumping up against the age-old ceiling that sends young actresses into semi-seclusion until they're ready to accept more venerable character roles. Some actresses would have declared victory, withdrawn from the field and gone on to regale their children with tales of Hollywood in its glory days.

Ball had other plans. Instead of retreating, she rolled up her sleeves, gathered her nerve and made remarkably bold decisions — displaying an audacity that led her to a singular

Lucille Ball set the bar very high in her depiction of Lucy, and she's remembered as the queen of comedy.

and life-changing encounter with her character Lucy Ricardo. Her bold decision would revolutionize the entertainment industry.

Ball went on to break barriers and cultural stereotypes as the first female chief executive of a major studio. She was, at one time, the highest-paid woman in Hollywood. In the decades after she breached the barricade for comediennes on television, a troop of talented protégés poured through the opening: Carol Burnett (who considered Ball a close friend and "mentor"), Eve Arden, Mary Tyler Moore, Roseanne Barr, Julia Louis-Dreyfus, Fran Drescher and Ellen DeGeneres, among many others.

Still, what we remember best is Lucy, whose deft combination of physical hilarity and glamorous appeal was as improbable as it was inspired. From any perspective, show-business history or cultural phenomenon, Ball's contributions to the American zeitgeist remain unmatched. More than 60 years later, we're still laughing.

BALL'S BEGINNINGS

Humor, however, was in short supply during Ball's childhood. Her family endured more than its fair share of catastrophes, failures and just plain bad luck. Her paternal grandfather was known to rustle cattle between failed business ventures; her other grandfather was sued into destitution over a shooting accident on his property that resulted in the death of a child.

By all accounts, she adored her father, a tall, handsome man who bequeathed her his sense of humor and little else before surrendering to typhoid fever in 1915. With her mother often traveling to support the family, Ball, not yet 4, felt deeply the absence of the man whose death was among her first memories. Shuffled from relative to relative, she lived a childhood torn asunder, as bleak as the hardscrabble landscape of her native western New York.

Frequently left to fend for herself and her younger brother, Ball learned self-sufficiency at an early age by taking charge of the house-

Ball's first major role in *Stage Door* (1937) didn't lead to the silver screen stardom she hoped for.

Lucille Ball (center) with Katharine Hepburn (left) and Ginger Rogers on-set during the filming of *Stage Door*.

hold. "Bossy she was, in charge she was," remembers her brother, Fred Ball, "but I accepted that." She cobbled together a home for the two of them, and for the rest of her life, family became the essential element in her recipe for happiness.

Though the ache of losing her father would never fully resolve itself, Ball soon realized that performing was a reliable way to garner attention — attention that somehow helped her manage her losses. Performing soon became the activity that most held her interest and motivated her pursuits.

A TASTE FOR STARDOM

Make no mistake; Ball set her sights on stardom. Failing as a drama student in New York City at the tender age of 15, she soon returned to Manhattan determined to prove her teachers wrong. Fashion modeling led to a stint as a Chesterfield Cigarette Girl. Ball then set off for Hollywood when an offer came to join the Goldwyn Girls, a troupe of chorines serving as the eye candy in *Roman Scandals*, Eddie Cantor's Depression-era movie.

In the battle for recognition with thousands of other "gladiators of glamour," Ball called on the lessons absorbed from childhood — she outworked, outwitted and outlasted her competition — and earned the right to join the Hollywood fantasy factory at $50 a week.

She offered herself up to the machinery of stardom, and they poured her into every mold. Hollywood never had a more willing piece of clay. Signed briefly to Columbia and then as a contract player with RKO, Ball earned her acting stripes, appearing in 24 movies before she ever saw her name in the credits.

In 1937, she broke through with a major part in an A-list hit, co-starring with Katharine Hepburn and Ginger Rogers in *Stage Door*. Still, few people in or out of the business took much notice. For much of the next decade, Ball starred in B-movie Westerns, mysteries, melodramas, noirish crime stories and even comedies without finding an audience or even a discernible identity.

She would later tell film historian Robert Os-

borne, in an astutely self-aware moment: "No matter how I get dressed up, I always look like the cigarette girl at the Trocadero."

Regardless of the part, she developed into a quick study and a keen observer. Making good use of her apprenticeship, she soaked up habits, tips and techniques from veterans like Irene Dunne and Carole Lombard.

While she slowly climbed the show business ladder, destiny had something in store for Ball.

MEETING ARNAZ

In 1940, she would headline the RKO movie version of a Broadway show called *Too Many Girls*. The film was a forgettable, not-quite flop. Fifth on the cast list, reprising his role from the stage production, was a Cuban bandleader named Desi Arnaz.

"You could see the fireworks and the sparks," said Ball's good friend Van Johnson, who also co-starred in both productions. "She fell in love with him and his accent and his dark, dark beauty."

At 29, Ball was five and a half years older and far more successful than Arnaz. Nonetheless, after a stormy six-month courtship, in 1940 they decided to marry, against all odds and a good deal of advice.

Ball's biographer, Kathleen Brady, author of

Lucille: The Life of Lucille Ball, wrote, "Desi appreciated Ball's independent streak and Ball, who had never really gotten enough attention, found herself with this man who was jealous, passionate … and this made for lots and lots of excitement. And lots of trouble, too."

After a whirlwind wedding and honeymoon, the reality of their show-business marriage immediately made itself felt. Arnaz continued to lead his band, crisscrossing the country in an endless stream of one-nighters, waking day after day to find he had been almost everywhere but home. Arguments between the newlyweds became more frequent.

Two years later, nothing had changed in their long-distance marriage. Alas, not much had changed in the Hollywood firmament, either. Ball finally got a break as the romantic heroine opposite rising star Henry Fonda in *The Big Street*. She got rave reviews from the critics. Hollywood and the public yawned, however.

Something did change, however — and it would prove to be seminal. In 1943, MGM bought Ball's contract from RKO and immediately cast her to star in the musical comedy *Du Barry Was a Lady*. Filmed in Technicolor, the role required Ball to dye her natural brunette locks a bright, brassy red. Although, she detested the color at first, it foreshadowed the most striking element of the Lucy look. She never changed it again.

Du Barry was a major hit and led to one other small change — this one in perspective. Some Hollywood pros began to notice something that should have been evident all along as the real root of Lucille Ball's talent: She was funny. Hilariously funny.

MASTER OF PHYSICAL COMEDY

Busby Berkeley, who directed Ball in *Roman Scandals*, did notice her early on, remarking that she was the only Goldwyn Girl willing to take a pie in the face.

Ball first met Arnaz on the set of *Too Many Girls* (1940), where they hit it off immediately and married six months later.

Ball with Henry Fonda in *Big Street* (1942).

Ball would take a pie in the face — or anything else her directors might dream up in search of a laugh. Cast in more than a dozen comedies during the mid- to late 1940s, she came alive in roles that called for physical hijinks and characters that allowed her to use her remarkable talent for mimicry and slapstick. Suddenly she was absorbed in roles that liberated her natural ability to make people laugh.

Of her performance in *The Fuller Brush Girl*, *Variety* wrote, "If there were ever any doubts as to Miss Ball's forte, *Fuller Brush Girl* dispels them. She is an excellent comedienne…"

If Ball lacked the romantic beauty of Maureen O'Hara or the sophisticated charm of Katharine Hepburn, it became clear she had something neither of them could begin to match: a face and body as elastic as putty and the willingness to do practically anything and everything in the service of comedy.

As biographer Brady noted, "The future Lucy Ricardo was slowly emerging, like a photograph in a developing bath."

Brady also reported that even Buster Keaton — the former silent film superstar, who was also working at MGM at the time — observed Ball's work and advised the studio head, Louis B. Mayer, that his star had a "unique gift."

OK TO BE FUNNY

There was just one problem: Nobody else was paying much attention. Regardless of Ball's success in comedic roles, the gospel according to Goldwyn and Mayer was clear: Beautiful women sell tickets; funny women do not.

Media critic Gerard Jones outlined her dilemma: "As Lucy was entering her late thirties, I think she had to realize that she wasn't going to get the big lead, glamour girl roles anymore. There were very few places to go at that age."

But there was one place: radio, where it didn't matter how old you were or how you looked. Radio was about voices. And though it was still developing, Ball already had a unique voice.

CBS called her with an invitation to join the cast of *My Favorite Husband*, a weekly CBS radio show. The program brought together a talented young team: writer/producer Jess Oppenheimer, writers Bob Carroll Jr. and Madelyn Pugh, and actor Richard Denning, an affable leading man type who, like Ball, came with respectable Hollywood credentials. They played a middle-class couple, Liz and George Cooper, whose lives were constantly upended by Liz's fondness for screwball schemes meant to jumpstart a show business career and, in the process, drive her banker husband crazy.

The first of 124 episodes debuted in July 1948 in front of a live audience, like most radio comedies at that time. Today's ubiquitous laugh track was not yet ubiquitous.

A live audience was a revelation for the movie star, and Ball embraced them like dear, old friends. She became animated in a way that she had not on Hollywood soundstages and quickly learned to take her cues from the audience, to trust their instincts and, after a time, her own. Ball perfected her comic timing with real laughter and, occasionally, real silence.

To keep the laughs coming, she began to play to the crowd. Although the listeners at home couldn't see her facial expressions and body language, they could certainly hear the response they generated. Those expressions would later become Lucy Ricardo's stock-in-trade.

While Ball was honing her comedic skills, working with her writers to fashion the first incarnation of the ditzy American housewife

Ball's performance in *The Fuller Brush Girl* (1950) opposite Eddie Albert (left) cemented her position as a comedienne.

with oversized dreams, there was a whole new technology working out its own wrinkles. Broadcasters and sponsors were in a mad scramble to get onboard the TV bandwagon, and content — then, as now — was king ... or queen, in Ball's case.

As the forerunner of what would one day be called the "Tiffany Network," CBS was looking to find gold in existing properties. After two successful seasons, any programmer could see the potential in *My Favorite Husband*. They pitched the idea to their star.

INVENTING LUCY

Ball had the intuition and foresight to solve the two most emotionally fraught problems in her life: how to keep her husband's wandering eye at home where he could focus it on her and how to start a family, a dream she had nurtured for nearly a decade. Although she had already suffered three miscarriages, she was confident that if she could just get Arnaz within arm's length, a happy home filled with children would follow.

So she agreed to the network's offer with one non-negotiable modification: that Arnaz be cast as her on-screen husband. Naturally, CBS said no. Who, they asked, would believe an American housewife married to a Cuban bandleader?

But if they thought Ball was going to cave without a fight, they must have been thinking about some other redhead. It wasn't a war exactly, but the Arnazes certainly waged an extended campaign. And when the smoke cleared, *I Love Lucy* was scheduled to shoot its first episode — waiting only until Ball delivered her long-awaited first child.

At almost 40 years old, she was exhilarated and extremely thankful — both for Lucie Désirée Arnaz, who made her debut on July 17, 1951, and for her new TV show, which filmed its first episode two months later on Sept. 8.

As he would for 180 subsequent episodes, Arnaz introduced his real-life/TV wife to the studio audience before the cameras rolled: "And now, the star of the show, the mother of my child, the vice president of Desilu Productions and my favorite redhead: Lucille Ball!"

By the time the cameras stopped rolling on that first episode, something magical happened — Lucille found Lucy.

She wasn't the only one making discoveries. There were three other actors cast in what would become a beloved ensemble. Katherine Brady nailed the formula for perfect chemistry: "There was patient Ethel, volatile Ricky, stolid Fred, and flighty, airy Lucy — sometimes couple against couple, sometimes the boys against the girls." Indeed, the dynamic of the conflict varied from episode to episode, but the laughs remained constant.

The creative team and crew, too, became more skilled and confident, especially when

Ball with her daughter Lucie and granddaughter Katharine.

No Longer a Hit

After *I Love Lucy,* Ball continued to work in television. Lucille Ball took her beloved character in front of the cameras three more times. But her enthusiasm for the work was waning, and so were the ratings.

From 1962 to 1968, she starred in *The Lucy Show*, which was a hit. After that, she decided she didn't want to continue with a series unless she could work with her two children, Lucie Arnaz and Desi Arnaz Jr. So, she helped create *Here's Lucy*, which ran from 1968 to 1974.

Though this show was meant to be somewhat different from past incarnations of the character, *Here's Lucy* still captured the essence of Lucy. While Ball's character had a different background and the producers wanted to get away from the other shows she had been a part of, some aspects of Lucy were preserved and shine through during the course of *Here's Lucy*.

Ball's last sitcom, *Life With Lucy*, aired in 1986, co-starring her longtime friend and foil, Gale Gordon. ABC mercifully canceled it less than two months into its run. "All Lucille wanted to do was work as an actress," film historian Robert Osborne said. "And all the public would ever buy her in was Lucy. And when they would no longer buy her as Lucy, that was the tragedy of her life." The audience began to wince watching a 75-year-old woman doing pratfalls. So, at that point, they stopped watching.

Ball refused to play Lucy anymore unless she could work on-screen with her children.

the network renewed the show for 13 additional episodes, and then another 13, and finally an entire season: 39 full episodes. By season's end, *I Love Lucy* was the top-rated show in television, and Ball received her first Emmy Award nomination — as Best Comedian/Comedienne.

The Arnazes/Ricardos would soon take us to yet another place where television had never gone before.

FROM CRISIS TO OPPORTUNITY

When Ball found herself pregnant with her second child in 1952, she and Arnaz assumed that they would have to walk away from their runaway hit. Their chief concern was for the cast and crew who would lose their jobs. Ball was especially conflicted, wanting to give Arnaz a son but reluctant to sacrifice everything they had built.

Television, still in its infancy, had a simple approach to pregnancy: It didn't exist. Actresses who got pregnant were fired. The conventional wisdom was that the American public would not accept something so intimate (code for "sex") in their living rooms (and bedrooms).

But where Ball and Arnaz saw disaster, producer Jess Oppenheimer saw a great opportunity. If Ball is going to have a baby, he said, so is Lucy Ricardo. Ball and Arnaz jumped at the idea. CBS — not so much.

As it turned out, sponsor Philip Morris liked having the top show in television pushing its product. CBS reluctantly decided to take a chance when Philip Morris president, Alfred Lyons, issued a memo to everyone. It read: "To whom it may concern: Don't #%@! with the Cuban!"

In the end, the only edict that CBS issued concerned the words "pregnant" or "pregnancy"— they could never be used. Instead, Lucy was "expecting."

CONNECTING WITH THE AUDIENCE

Perhaps we loved her so much because we identified with her. After all, while the Ricardos (and the Arnazes) were having babies, the rest of the country was, too. The post-World War II baby boom was on.

But, perhaps what we loved most about Lucy Ricardo was the intuitive, unspoken sense that if life was a struggle and troubles abounded, then our best possible response was laughter. And there was nothing — no pratfall, no humiliation, no indignity — that Ball would not endure to make us laugh.

Lucy Ricardo longed desperately to be a star, to shine on the stage, and was constantly frustrated by Ricky's objections and her own ill-conceived schemes. Her obsessions were sweeping ... and her failures? Spectacular!

But Lucille Ball? That was a redhead of a completely different color. *I Love Lucy* was renewed during its second season for $8 million, the most anyone had ever paid for a television show. *Time* put Ball on its cover. *TV Guide* also: 39 times, including the inaugural issue. Ball was nominated for 13 primetime Emmy Awards (not just for her role on *I Love Lucy*), winning four times.

A Good Friend

Even in her final moments, one good friend remembered Lucille Ball's positive energy and thoughtfulness. "She never missed sending me flowers on my birthday," said Carol Burnett, "[but] she was in the hospital that week ... and we were expecting her to be released ... I got up the next morning and turned on the news and ... there it was. She died on my birthday. And that afternoon, her flowers arrived for me."

Ball with her second husband, producer Gary Morton.

AFTER THE LIMELIGHT

But what flowed so effortlessly into our living rooms was the result of a lot of effort. In the end, perhaps it simply wore them out.

Fifteen years was a long time to keep up appearances. From the beginning, Ball and Arnaz encouraged the public to think that their real marriage was as happy as the TV version. But it wasn't.

CBS programming executive Mike Dann remembers, "Desi's extracurricular activities, in a small town like Hollywood, were not the best-kept secrets in the world. He was a notorious womanizer and a pretty good drinker."

When their marriage ended, America might have grieved, but no one who knew them was surprised. The final episode of *The Lucy-Desi Comedy Hour* was filmed on March 2, 1960. Ball filed for divorce the next day.

Fred Ball said of his older sister, "She was not someone who would ever say, 'I've done it all and there's nothing more to be accomplished,' and she was definitely not someone who would ever give up."

Ball had more laughter left to give, and we loved her for it, though perhaps a bit less as time went on. With Arnaz's encouragement (they remained friends), she dusted off her famous character, renamed her Lucy Carmichael, invited Vivian Vance to the party, and called it *The Lucy Show*. Ironically, CBS was now worried that the show wouldn't work without Arnaz.

But if you're Lucille Ball, a little network uncertainty is a minor deterrent. She steamrolled the skeptics, and her show ran for six award-winning seasons, earning better ratings in its last season than its first.

During that show's second season, Ball bought Arnaz's shares of the company that they had started together and suddenly found herself the president of one of Hollywood's biggest studios. And, once again, she embraced the challenge, running stockholder meetings and making decisions about which shows the company would green light for production. It is quite possible that, without Ball's guidance, *Mission: Impossible* would have remained in development and *Star Trek* might never have boldly gone anywhere.

A tough boss at work, Ball still longed to share her home and her life with a man. She remarried in 1961, this time to a loving, loyal man: comedian Gary Morton.

Even though, by all accounts, Ball and Morton had a solid marriage and business partnership for 27 years, many friends felt that the love between Ball and Arnaz was never quite over.

"I do not believe that Desi ever really left her life," CBS exec Mike Dann said.

Madelyn Pugh, one of the original writers from *I Love Lucy*, said about her Desilu bosses: "There was such a bond between them; it could never be broken." Ball and Arnaz had a warm, loving conversation on what would have been their 46th wedding anniversary. Two days later, Arnaz passed away. ▢

Thomas Wagner and his wife Pamela Mason Wagner produced Finding Lucy, *an American Masters PBS documentary about Lucille Ball's life and work. His favorite episode is "The Dancing Star" (Season 4, Episode 27).*

Ricky Ricardo

Desi Arnaz • March 2, 1917 – Dec. 2, 1986

The Bandleader

Desi Arnaz went from a life of privilege in Cuba to cleaning birdcages in Florida before hitting it big in music and then making television history.

BY THOMAS WAGNER

On an otherwise uneventful day in October 1951, a small cadre of radio and television professionals went to work in support of a somewhat insecure but notably ambitious star of Hollywood B movies — and transformed the character of television — forever.

Although she occupied center stage in that historic and groundbreaking debut, Lucille Ball forever after gave credit to one individual for making that moment possible — her on- and off-screen husband, Desi Arnaz.

Ball was right on the money. It was only later — after the spectacular success of *I Love Lucy* and their jointly owned company, Desilu Productions — that media historians began to give credit where it was long overdue. Arnaz helped to create much of the television industry we know today. In collaboration with his handpicked team, he invented situation comedy and unwittingly wrote the playbook

Desi Arnaz was an astute businessman who both effectively ran Desilu and served as a vital creative force on *I Love Lucy*.

Arnaz, a bandleader in real life, played a version of himself on the show.

of the founders of Bacardi Rum.

His paternal grandfather was a doctor famous for his part in the last land battle of the Spanish-American War. Assigned as medical support to Teddy Roosevelt's Roughriders, he dashed up San Juan Hill and into history in a battle that gave Cuba its independence from colonial Spain. All things considered, it was a family of no small distinction.

Despite the prestige attached to the Arnaz name, in his autobiography, Arnaz remembered getting up at dawn during summer vacations to labor on one of the family farms: milking cows, cleaning stables — doing "cowboy chores," as he called them fondly.

As it did for most young Cubans of privilege, life revolved around family and hard work, values that young Desi held close for the rest of his life. Those character traits were a legacy directly from his father, whom he remembered as very proud, generous to a fault and more than a little stubborn.

If Arnaz's father believed in an idea, he would overcome any obstacle to make it work. He also demonstrated a progressive, forward-thinking approach to his business pursuits. The first Cuban in his province to build a plant for pasteurizing milk, he also pioneered the use of refrigerated trucks for delivery. Perhaps it is not surprising that those qualities — tenacity and a talent for innovative problem-solving — took root in young Desi's character and, years later, helped him achieve so much.

FROM NOTHING TO BAND LEADER

Arnaz's infamous tenacity was tested at an early age. The Great Depression, which devastated the American economy, also broke the economies of Latin American nations. The Cuban Revolution of 1933, which ultimately brought the dictator Fulgencio Batista to power, sent mobs of angry Cubans into the streets. Seeking social and economic justice, they burned their way through the enclaves of the wealthy, indiscriminately destroying the property of friend and foe alike.

Arnaz's father was imprisoned for six months in Havana. Upon his release, he quickly organized an escape to Miami. He soon arranged for his son to follow. They left behind the smoking ruin of their home — and nearly everything they owned.

for the genre, a book so smart, so cleverly conceived, that much of it is still in use today.

So how did that happen? How did an émigré from Cuba, with almost no experience in the film business and none in the world of television become the most successful executive producer of the most highly rated program on television — a show that, in addition to its immense popularity, was universally recognized as setting the gold standard for innovation and technical excellence? You might think that someone's "got some 'splainin' to do."

CHARMED LIFE IN CUBA

Desiderio Alberto Arnaz y de Acha was born into a politically prominent and wealthy family. He enjoyed what can only be described as a charmed, nearly idyllic childhood. His father, a much-loved mayor of Santiago de Cuba, owned substantial land on which the family operated a dairy, cattle ranch and poultry-pig farm. Arnaz's mother was the daughter of one

Lucille Ball and Desi Arnaz (fourth and fifth from the left above) first worked together on *Too Many Girls* (1940).

Business Acumen

Joining Xavier Cugat's Orchestra was a giant step into big-time show business, and Desi Arnaz was determined to make the most of it. From the older musician, Arnaz learned showmanship, insight into American music preferences and how to arrange an evening's program for maximum dramatic effect.

More importantly, Cugat taught him the business end of the business: scheduling rehearsals, dealing with personnel (especially finicky band members), negotiating salaries and working with nightclub owners. For Arnaz, it was a master class taught by a master. Taking the lessons in, he remembered virtually everything, a pattern he would repeat over and over.

Arnaz was 16 when he disembarked from a ferryboat in Key West. He and his father arrived with nothing and survived by selling tiles, bananas and anything else that would put dinner on the table. For Arnaz, "anything else" included a turn cleaning out canary cages as his English slowly improved. In time, they were able to send for his mother.

Strange as it might seem in retrospect, it was completely by accident that Arnaz stumbled into the music business. His closest prior brush with entertaining was serenading his girlfriends with romantic songs, a ritual for most young Cuban men. Arnaz, as it turned out, exhibited quite a bit more aptitude for performing than his peers. Auditioning with a $5 pawnshop guitar, he landed a spot singing and playing with a dance band and soon figured out that entertaining was a lot more fun (and a lot more lucrative) than cleaning birdcages.

One night, Xavier Cugat, the renowned bandleader who for a decade built enthusiasm for Latin music across the U.S., spotted Arnaz

Pepito, the famous Spanish clown (right) and Arnaz's friend, was part of the roadshow to get *I Love Lucy* on the air and then made a guest appearance on the show.

in a Miami club and auditioned him for a spot in his band. Unschooled as Arnaz was (when asked for the key he wanted to sing in, he was forced to admit he didn't have a clue), Cugat was impressed with this diamond in the rough. After Arnaz graduated from high school, Cugat brought him to New York as the singer in Xavier Cugat's Orchestra.

His reputation growing, Arnaz, with Cugat's blessing, returned to Miami. But now, leading his own band, he began to nurture a performance personality, styling himself as the Cuban Maurice Chevalier. Of course, it didn't hurt his rising popularity that he had a boatload of charm, fiery good looks and a brand of sex appeal that scorched the imaginations of his female fans.

Always on the lookout for ways to increase his visibility and keep his audiences satisfied, he introduced the conga line in a club one night and soon everyone in Miami was snaking through nightclubs to the rhythm of the rumba. The conga caught the attention of a theatrical producer and, after an audition with director George Abbott, Arnaz was beating his conga drum and singing in the Broadway musical *Too Many Girls.*

Hired to reprise his role in the film version, Arnaz was basking in Hollywood sunshine and learning the difference between stage and screen when he found himself staring into the big, blue eyes of his co-star Lucille Ball. A small slice of the conversation as he remembered it:

Arnaz: "Do you know how to rumba, Lucille?"

Ball: "No, I've never learned."

Arnaz: "Would you like me to teach you how to rumba?"

Six months later, on Nov. 30, 1940, they were married.

Man in Charge

Having observed him for 10 years, Lucille Ball suspected that her husband had some acting chops and a little business savvy. That he would become one of the most respected and capable producers in Hollywood astonished her and everyone else. Ball's gamesmanship might have secured him the job, but Arnaz was clearly leading the charge from then on.

LUCY AND DESI ON THE ROAD

Arnaz's career as an actor did not exactly make headlines. He appeared in small parts in just seven pictures over the next decade. Ball's, on the other hand, took off like a rocket. Reluctantly, she stayed in Hollywood while he hit the road, leading the Desi Arnaz Orchestra on a seemingly endless tour of American nightclubs. He saw his new bride on a catch-as-catch-can basis. This living in limbo stretched on for nearly 10 years.

One phone call changed everything. Attempting to lure Ball into the new and untested world of television, CBS suggested adapting her successful radio show, *My Favorite Husband,* for the small screen. Lucille countered, agreeing with her bosses except for one condition: that the role of her husband go to Desi.

Initially, and quite predictably, the network balked. They were wary of Arnaz's inexperience as an actor and even more of what they expected to be audience skepticism about a Cuban married to an American housewife. Behind closed doors, CBS executives referred to Arnaz

as "the bongo boy." CBS's final response: The public will not buy it. They wouldn't budge.

Ball and Arnaz calmly set about changing the corporate minds. They initiated plans to plead their case to the public and prove the network wrong. Working through their own company, Desilu Productions, they arranged to be part of a neo-vaudeville variety show touring movie palaces in the summer of 1950 as the opening entertainment for first-run movies.

Everybody they knew lent a hand: Pepito, a world-famous Spanish clown (who also happened to be Arnaz's fishing buddy) gifted them his famous cello sketch and personally taught its intricacies to Ball. Jess Oppenheimer, Madelyn Pugh and Bob Carroll Jr., the writers from the radio show, reshaped Pepito's act to accommodate Arnaz. And the immortal Buster Keaton, an admirer of Ball's from their days at MGM, gave her personal instructions on how to handle the cello and her other props, lessons she would remember and apply for the rest of her career.

Mix in an old fedora, a threadbare tailcoat, Arnaz's exotic allure, his excellent orchestra and Ball's pitch-perfect timing — the result was something much more than the sum of its parts. She portrayed an annoying but lovable clown, hungering for a moment in the spotlight, and he was the perfect foil, a straight man for the ages. It proved magical, and the public and critics alike surrendered completely to their warmth, wit and chemistry.

BEHIND-THE-SCENES GENIUS

The road from that moment to the first broadcast of I Love Lucy still proved rough and full of potholes, but Arnaz's confidence and competence won the day. The CBS executives were shocked right out of their suits — first with his brilliance as a comic actor whose timing matched and perfectly complimented his comically dexterous co-stars. Counter to their expectations, the public adored him, his accent and his frantic fracturing of the English language ("I'll cross that bridge when I burn it").

The first of many problems began with CBS's insistence on producing and shooting the show from New York, like almost all television

programming at that time. Neither Ball nor Arnaz wanted to uproot their family (Ball was pregnant with their first child). Arnaz's solution turned out to be as shrewd a business deal as anyone had yet struck in the youthful television industry. He offered to produce the series in California and shoot it on film, ensuring pristine quality that could be aired anywhere at anytime with no loss in picture quality.

CBS countered that filming would entail additional costs. So the couple each agreed to a $1,000 weekly salary cut. In return for that cost-cutting concession, Desilu would own the programs outright. Because syndication had not yet entered the lexicon and no one attached any value to a program once it had been broadcast, CBS was happy to turn the production headache over to the Arnazes.

The deal Arnaz struck was remarkably prescient. The cash value of *I Love Lucy* in syndication is incalculable, but it is estimated that nearly 65 years after its debut, it is watched 24/7 somewhere on the planet.

Arnaz knew from Ball's radio experience that a live audience was crucial for her performance. No one had ever attempted to conquer the rigorous demands of shooting 35mm film with a noisy and sometimes distracted audi-

The family at Desi Jr.'s christening in 1953 (top). Ball and Arnaz on *the Ed Sullivan Show* in 1954.

ence in attendance, however. The next few months were remarkable. Arnaz, up to that moment a bandleader with a knack for business, suddenly had to find solutions to some very thorny problems.

He met the challenge as if he had been producing television for years. First, Arnaz assembled a formidable team, drawing largely on people Ball had successfully worked with during her 18 years as a Hollywood contract player. As production manager, Desi hired Al Simon, a veteran who had pioneered the three-camera technique for game shows. And to execute the complex movements and lighting necessary for the three cameras, Arnaz called on famed Hollywood cinematographer, Karl Freund.

Desilu rented studio space, and Arnaz jumped through the hoops required to satisfy fire and occupancy codes, having special floors laid so that the television cameras could roll smoothly and silently and personally going to every household in the neighborhood to secure releases for operating a theater.

Arnaz solved each problem as it arose and later attributed much of his success as a producer to never letting "no" be the end of a conversation. Never. As it turned out, "the bongo boy" was a television genius.

Only one question remained: Would anyone care about the antics of an obsessive redhead, her linguistically challenged husband and their frumpy-but-loyal neighbors?

They didn't have to wait long for an answer. A few episodes into the first season, municipalities began to report a drop in water and telephone usage from 9 to 9:30 p.m. on Mondays. You couldn't hail a cab in Manhattan during that half-hour because all the cabbies were on their *I Love Lucy* break. There were dozens of other indications that the Arnazes had launched a big hit — not least that CBS ordered a full season of new episodes.

AFTER LUCY

With the success of *I Love Lucy* and the stress of producing and performing for nearly a decade, Arnaz could have taken it easy. Instead, he put his back into executive producing other hit series, including *The Untouchables*, *The*

Arnaz with his second wife, Edith, at their wedding in 1963.

Mothers-In-Law and *The Lucy Show*, after his divorce from Lucille in 1960.

The end of their marriage took its toll. Ball and Arnaz never cut ties completely, though, and remained friends. In 1963, Arnaz married Edith Mack Hirsch and gradually eased into semi-retirement in Del Mar, Calif. He enjoyed the track and raced thoroughbreds raised on his own horse farm. He never quite managed to give up his Cuban cigars. Edith died in 1985, and once again, Arnaz faced life alone. He died a year later at age 69 from lung cancer.

In his later years, he occasionally spoke of the pride he felt for his work, especially his prime contribution to American pop culture, *I Love Lucy*. His pioneering solutions to television's early puzzles will be remembered if not by the general public then surely by the professionals who still benefit from his ingenuity. Among the trailblazing elements that are part of the show's history: Ricky and Lucy Ricardo were the first interracial married couple to appear on television, and Arnaz was the first Latin-American television star.

It is a remarkable legacy. Still, Arnaz would be the first to tell you what gratified him the most — he was the *I* in *I Love Lucy*. ❏

Meet the

FULL NAME: Lucille Esmeralda McGillicuddy Ricardo
BIRTHDAY: Aug. 6, 1921
HOMETOWN: West Jamestown, N.Y.
ANCESTRY: Scottish; her great-great-great-grandfather, Angus McGillicuddy, came from Kildoonan, a town in northern Scotland
EDUCATION: Jamestown High School in Celoron, N.Y.
GREATEST WISH: To be in pictures
FOIBLE: Master schemer
CHARACTER: Lucy is a hopeless romantic and a dreamer, dead-set on getting her way and breaking into Ricky's show at the Tropicana. She can't sing a lick, but she's actually quite a skilled performer and comedienne, demonstrating remarkable resourcefulness and ingenuity in her many plots and plans.

Though she did show some early promise in high school starring as Juliet in *Romeo and Juliet*, she never advanced much beyond this budding success, despite making it into her husband's show occasionally. Instead, she's a dedicated mother and wife, though her antics often cause Ricky to lose his temper. Interestingly, she failed Spanish in high school, which may contribute to her difficulties communicating with Ricky.

Though Lucy often argues with her husband and frequently defies him and schemes against him, they always end up making up and are deeply in love. They have one child together, Ricardo Alberto Fernando Ricardo y de Acha Jr., known as Little Ricky, who was born on Jan. 19, 1953.

Lucy loves to shop and has a fondness for stylish dresses and hair treatments. Her natural hair color is a mousy brown, but she has her hair dyed red every two weeks. She's met many famous celebrities, sometimes under precarious circumstances, and has achieved an infamous status among some movie stars. She's so starstruck, she often gets herself into trouble trying to ogle her idols.

Lucy's best friend, Ethel Mertz, is also her landlord — and later her tenant, when she and Ricky move to the countryside. Together, they've had all kinds of adventures. Lucy has traveled the world, going all over the United States, Mexico, the United Kingdom and Europe, including Italy, France, Switzerland, Monte Carlo and other places, as well, including Japan and Cuba.

Ricardos

FULL NAME: Ricardo Alberto Fernando Ricardo y de Acha III
BIRTHDAY: Uncertain but probably between 1917 and 1921
HOMETOWN: West Havana, Cuba
ANCESTRY: Cuban
EDUCATION: Havana University
GREATEST WISH: A family man, Ricky wants to keep his wife, Lucy, happy
FOIBLE: Short-tempered
CHARACTER: Ricky Ricardo is a performer, conga drummer, bandleader and eventual nightclub manager known for Cuban classics, including his signature "Babalu." He has a large extended family back in Cuba, but he left in 1938 and didn't go back to visit until 1956.

Raised on a cigar tobacco farm in Cuba, Ricky showed a talent for performing at an early age. His father often dispensed words of advice to him, which he later recounts

Ricky served in the Army at one point,

earning a Good Conduct Medal. After a blind date set up by Marion Strong with an attractive redhead, he fell head-over-heels in love. After marrying his paramour, Lucy, he settled in New York City — and later, Connecticut — and lived out the classic American dream.

Beyond his work as a bandleader, Ricky enjoys sports and playing cards. He's a devoted father, husband and friend to his neighbors the Mertzes. Ricky enjoys minor celebrity status and movie stardom, which offers Lucy multiple opportunities to rub elbows (and pies) with celebrities.

Ricky is given to fits of temper, and he has traditional notions about how his wife is supposed to behave. She often subverts his wishes, however, and Ricky has more than once had to deal with the ramifications of his wife's zany actions. Despite that, he unreservedly loves Lucy and does everything he can to make sure she is happy.

Ethel Mertz

Vivian Vance • July 26, 1909 – Aug. 17, 1979

The Best Friend

·····································

*After a successful theater career,
Vivian Vance reluctantly moved to television
to take on the role that made her famous.*

BY MARK GRIFFIN

"What do I want to get mixed up in that for? It's only a television show…" was Vivian Vance's initial reaction when *I Love Lucy* director Marc Daniels invited the actress to audition for the role of Ethel Mertz in 1951.

Playing second fiddle to Lucille Ball on television…whatever for? After all, Vance had already starred on Broadway and earned excellent reviews for her performances in musicals and melodramas alike. What's more, she had worked with some of the greatest theatrical talents in the business, including Ethel Merman, Cole Porter and Paul Muni. Why should she get mixed up with television, indeed?

"Vivian had some very impressive credits under her belt," says Vance biographer Alvin Walker, who co-authored *The Other Side of Ethel Mertz* with

In the episode "Lucy Gets a Paris Gown," Vivian Vance's comedic timing and chemistry with Lucille Ball shine through in her performance.

Vance was a seasoned stage veteran before playing Ethel.

Frank Castelluccio. "She was a fine actress, adept at comedy, drama and musical theater. Vivian had damn near perfect timing and was known for delivering the goods. ... The moment she hit New York, she started cultivating her appearance and over time emerged as a glamorous chanteuse, singing in supper clubs and performing on Broadway." It was the kind of sophisticated theatrical life that Vance had dreamed about since she was a little girl.

DETERMINED FROM THE START

Vivian Roberta Jones was born in 1909 in Cherryvale, Kan., and from the beginning, she knew exactly what to do to maintain her place in the spotlight. "Vivian was very funny," her older sister Venus once remarked. "Vivian was already quite comical when she was just two and three years old."

After her family relocated to Independence, Kan., Vance became increasingly interested in acting, and her near obsession with performing was encouraged by her high school drama teacher. Cast as an elderly Asian man in

Beyond Ethel

Unlike her *I Love Lucy* co-star William Frawley, who popped up in more than 100 movies, Vivian Vance made appearances in only four films.

Take a Chance (1933) — Vance was uncredited as one of the dancehall girls.

The Secret Fury (1950) — Vance has a supporting role in this gripping whodunit starring Claudette Colbert and Robert Ryan. Also appearing in the film is Vance's third husband, Philip Ober.

The Blue Veil

The Blue Veil (1951) — Vance and Ober next appeared together in this rarely screened melodrama starring Jane Wyman (above left) and Charles Laughton (above right).

The Great Race (1965) — Vance has a glorified cameo as suffragette Hester Goodbody in director Blake Edwards' homage to silent film comedies. When Vance attended a preview screening of the film, she remarked, "I had more costumes than lines."

a school production of *East is West*, a disguised Vance gave such a convincing performance that her own father didn't recognize her in the role.

In an uncanny similarity to the challenges faced by her future *I Love Lucy* co-star William Frawley, Vance pursued her acting ambitions under the disapproving eye of her mother, Mae, who was described as "devoutly and dogmatically religious." In later years, Vance would reveal that the pursed lips expression that she sometimes employed in her Ethel Mertz characterization was partly borrowed from her mother.

Despite her mother's misgivings, Vance was determined to pursue a career in show business. Before leaving Kansas, she adopted a marquee-friendly stage name — Vivian Vance — after Vance Randolph, a colleague in the local theater scene.

NEW YORK, CHICAGO AND A BREAKDOWN

After a brief first marriage, Vance went to Manhattan in 1932. Once in New York, she studied drama with the legendary stage actress Eva Le Gallienne. While this training was invaluable, it didn't immediately help Vance find work. The rejections and indifference of stone-faced casting directors caused Vance to start second guessing her abilities.

"When I got to New York, I found I wasn't as good as my friends thought I was," she recalled. "But of course, I couldn't go back."

In 1933, Vance married her second husband, violinist George Koch. While Koch provided some financial stability for the aspiring actress, the couple was not well matched and Vance remained single-mindedly focused on furthering her career.

From the chorus of Oscar Hammerstein and Jerome Kern's *Music in the Air*, Vance went on to understudy Ethel Merman's Reno Sweeney in Cole Porter's musical production *Anything Goes*. Later there was a bit part in Porter's *Red, Hot, and Blue!* Although she was racking up credits on Broadway, Vance hadn't achieved the kind of important breakthrough that would propel her to top billing.

Then, in 1937, Vance's big break finally arrived. *Hooray For What!*, an anti-war musical, seemed to have everything going for it: Vincente Minnelli was the director, Agnes de Mille was the choreographer and the score was courtesy

Lucille Ball insisted that Vance join her on *The Lucy Show*.

of Harold Arlen and E.Y. Harburg, who would go on to compose the songs for *The Wizard of Oz*. Originally cast as a singing spy was future MGM arranger and *Eloise* author Kay Thompson. Although Thompson received positive notices during tryouts in Boston, she was fired and replaced by her understudy: Vivian Vance. Initially the plan called for Vance to cover the role until a replacement could be found, but Vance performed so expertly that the producers decided to let her finish out the Broadway run.

In 1945, Vance joined the Chicago company of *The Voice of the Turtle*, and the experience would dramatically alter the course of her life. While she was acclaimed for her performance in the John Van Druten drama, ominous signs of emotional illness began to appear. During a performance, Vance reached for a prop but found that she was completely immobilized. "It was one of the most sickening moments I have ever gone through," she remembered. Later Vance recalled "weeping hysterically for

> *"She was a good-looking woman and a stately lady and to place her in the frumpy Ethel Mertz clothing and hair-dos, it was demeaning especially because Vance saw other possibilities for herself."*
>
> — author Audrey Kupferberg

causes I did not know … I was positive I was losing my mind."

After her debilitating breakdown, Vance took a two-year break from acting. Through analysis and with the support of her third husband, actor Philip Ober, Vance eventually regained her health. In 1951, actor-director Mel Ferrer staged a production of *The Voice of the Turtle* at the La Jolla Playhouse in California and of-fered Vance an opportunity to reprise her role. One evening, director Marc Daniels brought Desi Arnaz to a performance. As the first act concluded, Arnaz reportedly commented, "I think we've found Ethel." After expressing some initial trepidation, Vance agreed to join the cast of *I Love Lucy* at $350 a week.

PLAYING ETHEL

Initially, Vance was contracted for 13 weeks with the understanding that she could be written out of the show at any time. To play the dowdy Ethel Mertz, Vance would be paired with the much older William Frawley, de-glamorized and encouraged to maintain a fuller figure. "I don't think all of this sat very well with her," wrote *Meet the Mertzes* author Audrey Kupferberg. "She was a good-looking woman and a stately lady and to place her in the frumpy Ethel Mertz clothing and the hair-dos, it was demeaning especially because Vance saw other possibilities for herself. But at the same time, *I Love Lucy* really made her career."

Though Vance and Frawley didn't get along, their off-screen ire served to make their characters seem more realistic.

Vance had many opportunities to display the full range of her talents on *I Love Lucy*. "My favorite episode is 'The Housewarming' (season 6, episode 23)," says biographer Walker. "Ethel is jealous of Lucy's friendship with neighbor Betty Ramsey (Mary Jane Croft). There's a scene in which the girls are having lunch and Vivian plays anger, sarcasm and surprise almost at the same time and with perfect timing and amazing reactions."

After *I Love Lucy* and *The Lucy-Desi Comedy Hour* concluded their enormously successful nine-year run in 1960, executive producer Desi Arnaz offered Vance and Frawley a once-in-a-lifetime opportunity — their own spin-off series. Instead of hamming it up as second bananas, Frawley and Vance could be the principal characters. "Vivian quickly vetoed this idea," says Walker. "She feared she would have another nervous breakdown if she had to work with Frawley again … no amount of money was enough. The spin-off series would have been a great money-maker for Frawley and when he found out that Vivian had refused, it further cemented his disdain for her."

In 1962, Lucille Ball launched a new sitcom entitled *The Lucy Show*, and although Vivian Vance was now married to her fourth husband and living in Connecticut, Ball insisted that Vance join her for this new venture. The show was an instant hit, lasting six seasons. Although Vance bowed out after three years, she would continue to make occasional guest appearances. One of these episodes, in which Ball and Vance encounter Oscar-winning legend Joan Crawford, is considered an all-time fan favorite.

AFTER LUCY

After *The Lucy Show*, Vance resumed her theater work and accepted a role as a suffragette in director Blake Edwards' comedy *The Great Race* (1965) with Natalie Wood, Tony Curtis and Jack Lemmon. In 1975, Vance was featured in a memorable guest spot on the hit television series *Rhoda*. Many of Vivian Vance's fans hoped that she would become a regular on that sitcom, but Vance was battling cancer by that time.

Vance reunited with Ball one last time for the CBS special *Lucy Calls the President* (1977). "Vivian was very brave," remembered

Vance guest starred on the TV series *Rhonda* in 1975.

co-star Gale Gordon. "She knew she had cancer and never said anything to anybody." In August 1979, Vance died at the age of 70 in Belvedere, Calif. Upon learning of Vance's passing, Ball commented, "I lost one of the best friends I've ever had, and the world has lost one of the great performers of the stage, films and television."

In an interview given not long before her death, Vance seemed to have revised her earlier opinions about "getting mixed up" with a television show. Reflecting on the series that had endeared her to millions of viewers, Vance said, "My introduction to *I Love Lucy* was one of those fortunate happenings that actors only dream about." 📺

Mark Griffin is the author of A Hundred or More Hidden Things: The Life and Films of Vincente Minnelli *as well as a forthcoming biography of Rock Hudson to be published by HarperCollins. His favorite episode is "In Palm Springs"* (see page 35).

Fred
Mertz

William Frawley • Feb. 26, 1887 – March 3, 1966

The Landlord

....

The vaudevillian and ultimate character actor, William Frawley lobbied hard for his role in I Love Lucy.

BY MARK GRIFFIN

Although he had been a vaudeville star, appeared on Broadway and turned up in more than 100 films dating back to the silent era, William Frawley didn't become a household name until he was cast as the irascible, penny-pinching landlord Fred Mertz in *I Love Lucy*.

After CBS committed to a weekly television series starring Lucille Ball and Desi Arnaz as a scheming redhead and her bandleader husband, the search was on to find a couple of actors to play their neighbors — curmudgeonly Fred and his long-suffering wife, Ethel.

Initially, Ball hoped to cast Gale Gordon and Bea Benaderet as the squabbling Mertzes. This pair of dependable actors had played similar roles on Ball's CBS radio program, *My Favorite Husband*.

Though Frawley was a seasoned performer and took his role as Fred Mertz seriously, he stuck to himself on-set, often staying in his dressing room.

Frawley was cast alongside George Raft (left) in the film *Bolero* (1934). Frawley acted in more than 100 films during his career.

As both Gordon and Benaderet were contractually tied to other ventures, the *I Love Lucy* team continued looking for a seasoned duo to play Fred and Ethel.

BORN TO PLAY

From the moment he learned that *I Love Lucy* was going into production, William Frawley wanted in. Though there were some legitimate concerns raised regarding his casting, Frawley was accustomed to overcoming obstacles.

Born in 1887 in Burlington, Iowa, Frawley discovered at an early age that he loved to perform. Whether he was singing in the St. Paul's Catholic Church choir or playing bit parts at the Burlington Opera House, Frawley felt right at home.

However, Frawley's devoutly Catholic mother, Mary, was dead set against her son pursuing any sort of a career in show business. Instead of a son hamming it up in the spotlight, Mary envisioned her "Bill" as a stenographer for the Union Pacific Railroad. Attempting to placate his domineering mother, Frawley took the job, though co-workers remembered him humming and singing ragtime tunes while he worked.

Frawley's position with the railroad brought him to Chicago, where he landed a role in the chorus of the musical stage comedy *The Flirting Princess*. At 21, Frawley was exactly where he wanted to be, but his mother adamantly refused to see the show. "My mother sent a note … saying that she'd rather plant flowers on my grave than see me on the stage," Frawley recalled years later.

Migrating west, Frawley secured a solo singing engagement at the Rex Café in Denver. For $23 a week, he belted out songs like "Waiting for the Robert E. Lee." Teaming up with pianist Franz Rath, Frawley put together an act called "A Man, A Piano and a Nut." Frawley's Irish tenor voice was a crowd pleaser, and some historians believe he was among the first entertainers to perform such standards as "My Melancholy Baby" and "Carolina in The Morning."

FROM VAUDEVILLE TO PICTURES

Decades before he achieved fame as Fred Mertz, Frawley was part of another successful show business partnership. After marrying Edna Louise Broedt in 1914, the couple toured as "Frawley and Louise," which has been described as "one of the great comedy acts of vaudeville." After Broedt divorced Frawley in 1927, the actor never married again.

Once he signed a contract with Paramount Pictures in 1937, Frawley became one of the most in-demand character actors in Hollywood, offering able support to such stars as James Cagney, Bette Davis and Carole Lombard. He made memorable appearances in a range of films, including *Something to Sing About* (1937), *The Adventures of Huckleberry Finn* (1939) and *Rose of Washington Square* (1939).

The 1940s proved to be an especially prolific decade for Frawley with pivotal roles in some major movies. In director William Wellman's *Roxie Hart* (1942), he plays a bartender

Mertz Alert

Before he became synonymous with Fred Mertz and *I Love Lucy*, William Frawley was one of the busiest character actors in Hollywood. Here is just a sampling of some of the movies in which he appeared during his long and varied career.

Lord Loveland Discovers America (1916) — Frawley made his screen debut as Tony Kidd in this silent film about an Englishman who sets off for America to wed a wealthy heiress.

The Lemon Drop Kid (1951)

The Lemon Drop Kid (1934) — In one of his best early film roles, Frawley plays fast-talking William Dunhill. In 1951, more than 17 years later, Frawley (above left) appeared in the remake of this Damon Runyon tale with Bob Hope (center) in the lead role and co-starring Marilyn Maxwell (right).

Three Cheers for Love (1936) — In this lighthearted Paramount musical, Frawley plays a character named Milton Shakespeare.

The General Died at Dawn (1936) — Frawley is the drunken arms dealer Mr. Brighton in this Oscar-nominated Gary Cooper classic.

The Bride Came C.O.D. (1941) — Frawley's Sheriff McGee gets tangled up with flier James Cagney and an eloping heiress played by Bette Davis.

Ziegfeld Follies (1946) — In this lavish MGM extravaganza, Frawley appears with Fanny Brice and Hume Cronyn in a comedy sequence entitled "A Sweepstakes Ticket." Lucille Ball tames a pack of slinky cat women in the elaborate opening number, "Here's to the Girls."

Monsieur Verdoux (1947) — Frawley is police inspector Jean La Salle in this classic comedy directed by Charlie Chaplin.

Easter Parade (1948) — Judy Garland and Fred Astaire are the stars of this song-packed Irving Berlin musical. Frawley appears briefly as a police officer who tickets playboy Peter Lawford.

Rancho Notorious (1952) — Frawley made one of his final film appearances as Baldy Gunder in this gothic Western directed by Fritz Lang and starring Marlene Dietrich.

Frawley played "Bub" O'Casey on the TV series *My Three Sons (left)*. In *Desire* (1936), Frawley played alongside Gary Cooper (right).

harboring fond memories of brassy jailbird Ginger Rogers. In the Christmas classic *Miracle on 34th Street* (1947), Frawley took on the roll of a cigar-chomping advisor to the judge presiding over Kris Kringle's competency trial. However, by the early 1950s, Frawley found himself appearing in B-pictures like *Kill the Umpire* (1950) and *Abbott and Costello Meet The Invisible Man* (1951).

"I don't mind admitting my movie career was having a bit of a lull when *Lucy* came along," Frawley recalled.

FOOT IN THE DOOR

One evening in 1951, an expectant Lucille Ball received an unexpected call from the 64-year-old Frawley. Although Ball and Frawley had both appeared in MGM's all-star extravaganza *Ziegfeld Follies* (1946), they had not shared scenes together. Citing his extensive experience playing cantankerous characters in dozens of movies, he expressed interest in playing Fred Mertz. Ball immediately recognized that the grump next door was a role that Frawley seemed born to play.

"He *was* Fred Mertz," Ball later remarked. "The writers took Bill Frawley verbatim." Ball and Arnaz were eager to cast Frawley, but CBS executives weren't nearly as enthusiastic.

"Lucy wanted him because he would have been perfect for the part, but Frawley presented some problems," said Rob Edelman, who collaborated with Audrey Kupferberg on *Meet the Mertzes* about William Frawley and Vivian Vance. "Frawley was getting up there in age ... [and] had developed a reputation as a drinker. Was he going to be irresponsible? He was told straight up by Desi Arnaz, 'You will show up on time. You will be professional. If we have any problems, you're out.' So, Frawley basically got himself together and he was fine."

While Frawley would affectionately refer to Ball as "that kid" and formed a lasting friendship with Arnaz, there was no love lost between Frawley and Vance, who was 22 years younger than her on-screen husband.

"The two of them were superb as Fred and Ethel and they were hilarious together," Edelman said. "But from the get go, it was like oil and water."

What was the source of their antagonism? "I think it had something to do with Frawley's animosity toward many women," Kupferberg said. "He had one marriage in real life that was unsuccessful. He didn't seem to warm up to a lot of women. And I think Vance felt that. I think she was a rather fragile personality and Frawley just played on her fragility."

ANIMOSITY OFF-SCREEN

Things between the two got off on the wrong foot almost immediately, according to Alvin Walker, co-author of the Vance bio, *The Other Side of Ethel Mertz*. "Early in the series, Bill Frawley had overheard Vivian complaining about being matched up with someone so much older than she," Walker said. "She reportedly referred to him as an 'old coot' and the relationship snowballed downhill from there. ... There are a few episodes where she had to kiss Frawley and if you watch closely, you can see that she doesn't even touch his lips. She basically hated the guy."

It didn't help matters when Vance became the first performer to win an Emmy Award as Best Supporting Actress in a Comedy in 1954. Frawley, who was nominated as Best Supporting Actor several times during the run of the series, never won. The outspoken Frawley wasn't exactly gracious about going home empty handed, either. "It didn't surprise me," he grumbled. "I knew they didn't know what they were doing when Vivian Vance got one!"

Several *I Love Lucy* episodes paid tribute to Frawley's roots as a vaudevillian. In "Ricky Loses His Voice" (season 2, episode 9), Lucy and the Mertzes fill in for him at a Tropicana opening. Fred dusts off an old script from his touring days, "Flapper Follies of 1927," and he and Ethel perform "Carolina in the Morning," which Frawley claimed to have introduced. In "Mertz and Kurtz" (season 4, episode 2), Fred reunites with vaudeville partner Barney Kurtz. Back in the 1920s, their comedy act had been billed as "Laugh Till It Hurts with Mertz and Kurtz." In episodes like these, viewers were given a sense of what a charismatic and versatile performer Frawley must have

been during his vaudeville days.

After the unprecedented success of *I Love Lucy* and nine seasons of playing Fred Mertz, Frawley would go on to co-star in the sitcom *My Three Sons*, opposite Fred MacMurray. For his final film, *Safe at Home!* (1962), Frawley, a lifelong baseball fanatic, was thrilled to share the screen with New York Yankees legends Mickey Mantle and Roger Maris.

A year before Frawley died of a heart attack in 1966, he reunited with Lucille Ball one last time. For an episode of Ball's post-*I Love Lucy* series, *The Lucy Show*, Frawley played a cranky, no-nonsense horse trainer. Upon meeting him, Lucy does the ultimate double take and says, "You know, he reminds me of someone I used to know ..." 📺

The sports comedy *Safe at Home!* (1962) featured Frawley in a supporting role.

FULL NAME: Ethel Louise Roberta Mae Potter Mertz
BIRTHDAY: Sometime between 1905 and 1915
HOMETOWN: Albuquerque, N.M.
ANCESTRY: Unknown, possibly English or Dutch
EDUCATION: Albuquerque Elementary School, high school unknown
GREATEST WISH: To get some excitement in her life
FOIBLE: Gossip and snoop
CHARACTER: Ethel Mertz was raised outside of Albuquerque on a ranch. She met Fred Mertz when she was 19, and the pair eloped, beginning a successful career in vaudeville.

Ethel is a talented singer and dancer and has a wonderful soprano voice. In her younger days, she was crowned Miss Albuquerque, and she is well liked and respected in her home town. She toured and performed with Fred for a number of years before settling down in New York City.

Her marriage to Fred has become difficult in some respects, and she's complained that she was a catch in her younger days, with men fawning over her. Though she resents her husband's cheapness, she and Fred do love one another. She's especially fond of her neighbors the Ricardos, and she is godmother to Little Ricky.

Her best friend, Lucy, often gets Ethel in trouble, but she's happy to have the excitement, too. Ethel and Lucy constantly back one another up and help each other in various schemes and adventures.

However, occasionally the two compete with one another, especially when it comes to show business. Ethel is naturally more talented than Lucy as a performer, which Lucy resents, but the two always make up and remain steadfast friends.

When the Ricardos move to Westport, Conn., Ethel is devastated and can't bear life without her closest friend. When the Mertzes arrange to move into the Ricardos' new guesthouse permanently, their old landlord-renter relationship is turned on its head.

Meet the

FULL NAME: Frederick Hobart Mertz
BIRTHDAY: 1888
HOMETOWN: Steubenville, Ohio
ANCESTRY: Irish
EDUCATION: Unknown
GREATEST WISH: Never to spend a dime
FOIBLE: Cheap, a penny pincher
CHARACTER: Though Fred Mertz has settled into a somewhat cantankerous though comfortable life with his wife, Ethel, he was something of a dynamo in his younger days. Making it to the rank of corporal in the U.S. Army, Fred was a Golden Gloves Boxing Champion in 1909 and a long-time vaudeville performer, touring the country as part of an act called "Mertz & Kurtz."

After meeting Ethel, the couple spent a year together before they eloped, as Fred was not popular with Ethel's father, Mr. Potter. After the wedding, the couple started a successful career in vaudeville, adapting their act and taking the name "Mertz & Mertz."

Fred is a talented performer, and during his time touring he would tap dance, sing and perform various comedic routines. He and Ethel probably toured around the country performing and working other jobs for about five years. Then they settled in New York City and bought a brownstone apartment building, where they met their eventual best friends, the Ricardos.

Though a relatively successful landlord, Fred lost his life's savings in the stock market crash of 1929, and this may be why he's so tight with money. During Fred's performing career, he managed his own act, and this earns him a spot as Ricky's band manager when the couples travel to Europe.

Fred's relationship with his wife is complicated, and the two often bicker, mostly about money. But Fred loves Ethel. He's also a devoted friend and godfather to the Ricardos' son. When the Ricardos move to Westport, Conn., both Fred and Ethel are dismayed at the loss of their best friends and promptly make an arrangement to take care of the Ricardos' chickens in exchange for free room and board and a share of the revenue from the eggs.

Lucy's FAMILY

Lucille Ball and Desi Arnaz's legacy lives on through their children, Lucie and Desi Jr.

BY GILLIAN G. GAAR

L ucille Ball and Desi Arnaz were married for more than 10 years before having two children — giving a younger generation its own "Lucie and Desi."

FIRST A DAUGHTER

Ball was one month shy of turning 40 when Lucie Désirée Arnaz was born on July 17, 1951, in Los Angeles. Ball had miscarried three times before finally giving birth to her first, much-longed-for child. Just three months later, *I Love Lucy* debuted on CBS.

Lucie made her TV debut on *The Lucy Show* and also appeared in her mother's subsequent series, *Here's Lucy*. The multi-talented Lucie has worked in television and film and on stage. She's made guest appearances in such hit shows as *Fantasy Island*, *Law & Order* and

The Arnaz family, Lucie (left) Desi, Lucille and Desi Jr. in 1959, one year before the couple divorced.

Murder, She Wrote as well as numerous made-for-TV movies. In 1985, she starred in her own TV show, *The Lucie Arnaz Show*, playing a psychologist with a call-in radio show. Though a similar idea would prove to be a great success for Kelsey Grammer in *Frasier*, Lucie's show ran for only six episodes before being canceled. Her film work includes 1977's *Billy Jack Goes to Washington* (which is loosely based on Frank Capra's *Mr. Smith Goes to Washington*); Neil Diamond's film, *The Jazz Singer* (1980); and most recently the animated film *Henry & Me* (2014).

Lucie has been especially successful in theater. Her performance in the 1979 musical *They're Playing Our Song* won her a Theatre World Award, Los Angeles Drama Critics Circle Award and Outer Critics Circle Award; in 1986, she won the prestigious Sarah Siddons Award for her performance in the touring production of *My One and Only*. In 2014, she appeared in a touring production of the musical *Pippin*. Lucie also performed in her own nightclub act and released her first album, *Just in Time*, in 2010.

She's been extensively involved with promoting her parents' legacy. Lucie won an Emmy as co-executive producer (along with her husband, actor Laurence Luckinbill) of the 1993 television documentary *Lucy and Desi: A Home Movie*, and she co-wrote and directed a one-woman touring show about her mother, *An Eve-*

The band Dino, Desi & Billy appear on *The Dean Martin Show*. Pictured with Martin are Billy Hinsche (left), Desi Arnaz Jr. and Dean "Dino" Martin Jr. (right).

Lucie Arnaz at the 5th Annual TV Land Awards in 2007.

ning with Lucille Ball: Thank You For Asking.

Lucie was married to actor Phil Vandervort from 1971 to 1977. Since 1980, she has been married to actor Laurence Luckinbill, and together they have three children, Simon, Joseph and Katharine.

THEN A SON

Desiderio Alberto Arnaz IV was born on Jan. 19, 1953, in Los Angeles — the same date the *I Love Lucy* episode depicting the birth of his fictional counterpart, Little Ricky, aired. Like his sister, Desi (who shortened his name to Desi Arnaz Jr.) appeared in his mother's show *Here's Lucy.*

But he first made his name in music when he was 12 as a drummer in the pop group Dino, Desi & Billy — "Dino" was Dean Paul Martin, Dean Martin's son, and Billy Hinsche later was a musician for The Beach Boys. The group recorded under Frank Sinatra's label, Reprise, and had Top 40 hits in 1965 with "I'm a Fool" and "Not the Lovin' Kind."

Desi then moved into TV (*The Streets of San Francisco* and *Love, American Style*) and film (the Western *Billy Two Hats* and *Joyride*, which

co-starred Robert Carradine). He also starred in the short-lived series *Automan*. He appeared as a musical guest on the Feb. 21, 1976, episode of *Saturday Night Live*, which was hosted by his father. He went on to portray his father in the 1992 film *The Mambo Kings.*

In 1986, Desi moved to Boulder, Colo., where he purchased and restored the Boulder Theater, home to the Boulder City Ballet Company. Desi has also produced a number of shows at the venue, including a return of his pop group, Ricci, Desi & Billy — Ricci is another of Dean Martin's sons, replacing his brother Dino, who died in 1987.

Desi was married to actress Linda Purl from 1980 to 1981. He married his second wife, Amy Bargiel, in 1987 and legally adopted her daughter, Haley, from her first marriage. Amy died of cancer on Jan. 23, 2015. Prior to both marriages, Desi became a father when his girlfriend, Susan Howe, gave birth to a daughter, Julia Arnaz.

Lucie and Desi have also worked together on projects commemorating their parents. They co-executive produced the *I Love Lucy 50th Anniversary Special* in 2001. Both appeared in *Babalu: The American Songbook Goes Latin*, a celebration of the music of the Desi Arnaz Orchestra, which was also created and directed by Lucie. The show premiered in New York City in 2010 and has since been performed in other cities. 📺

In *Mambo Kings* (1992), Desi Arnaz Jr. plays his father alongside Antonio Banderas (left) and Armand Assante (right).

"I LOVE Lucy"

TIDBITS & TRIVIA

Superstar Guest Stars

I Love Lucy and later *The Lucy-Desi Comedy Hour* featured many big-name guest stars, especially during the time the Ricardos and Mertzes were in Hollywood during seasons 4 and 5. Some of the A-listers they met include William Holden, Eve Arden, Cornel Wilde, Van Johnson, Harpo Marx, Richard Widmark, Rock Hudson and John Wayne.

In later episodes, Charles Boyer, Bob Hope and Orson Welles encountered the zany redhead.

Actors who guest-starred in *The Lucy-Desi Comedy Hour* include Tallulah Bankhead, Danny Thomas and the cast of *Make Room for Daddy*, Maurice Chevalier, Milton Berle, Betty Grable, Fernando Lamas, Cesar Romero, Fred MacMurray, Red Skelton, Howard Duff and Ernie Kovacks.

The episode
"Lucy Goes to the Hospital"
aired on

Jan. 19, 1953

About 12 hours before the broadcast, Lucille Ball gave birth to Desi Arnaz Jr.

Lucille Ball was considered for the role of Scarlett O'Hara in *Gone With the Wind*.

Though Lucy and Ethel are supposed to be further apart in age, Lucille Ball was only

2 YEARS YOUNGER
than Vivian Vance.

Real-Life Marriage

Lucille Ball and Desi Arnaz were married on Nov. 30, 1940, and divorced in 1960. She was six years older than him, but because it was frowned upon at the time for a woman to be older than her husband, on the marriage certificate, she claimed to be three years younger and he claimed to be three years older.

I Love Lucy was filmed from start to finish, and reshoots were rare.